Luther 500

Five talks to commemorate the origins of the Reformation

St Peter's Methodist Church, Canterbury, 27 September - 25 October 2017

Edited by John Butler

Copyright © 2017 Canterbury and East Kent Methodist Circuit and The Diocese of Canterbury.

ISBN: 9781973595274

Contents

Preface
by the Rt. Revd. Trevor Willmott, Bishop of Dover.

'If I knew the world was to end tomorrow, I would plant a tree today'. Of all that Martin Luther wrote and said, these words resonate strongly with me and, I would hope, with the whole Christian Church as we continue to seek and to bear out witness to Jesus Christ and to serve the needs of His world. Luther sought to draw the Church back to its primary purposes - to be a community of believers open and inclusive of all and to be the agent through which God's ongoing purposes in Christ be shared and lived by the whole world.

At a time when our world faces many challenges, and anxiety is increasingly at the top of individuals' and communities' agendas, Luther's words pull all of us to a renewed hope in Jesus Christ.

For all of us who were privileged to share in Luther Conversations in St Peter's Methodist Church, Canterbury, the generous self-giving of the speakers will have reflected something of that rooted hope in Jesus Christ. The publication of the talks in this e-book will, I hope, enable us to continue the conversations as together we seek to embody the promise of new life which God has given to all of us in Jesus.

For the privilege given to all of us of sharing in the rich conversations, we owe an enormous debt of gratitude to Harvey Richardson and to his team, not only for organising time together but, more importantly, for having the vision to draw us together as brothers and sisters in Christ.

With my prayers and blessing
+Trevor

Introduction

by Revd. Harvey Richardson, Supernumerary Minister
Canterbury & East Kent Circuit of the Methodist Church

In the summer of 2015 a few friends from different Christian churches in and around Canterbury met over lunch to discuss their shared concerns about the current state of Christian belief and the future of organised religion in Britain. Gradually the idea emerged of trying to bring these concerns into the public domain as a local way of commemorating the 500th anniversary of the Protestant Reformation in 2017. The fanciful idea of nailing 95 modern theses to the doors of Canterbury Cathedral rapidly gave way to the far more sensible suggestion of a forum for the public discussion of our concerns.

It seemed to us that there is so much confusion and misunderstanding, both within and outside the church, about the doctrines of Christianity and their relevance in today's world that the time was right for just such a public conversation. It seemed right, too, that the project should have an ecumenical sponsorship, and to that end the Canterbury and East Kent Methodist Circuit joined forces with the Anglican Diocese of Canterbury to carry forward the planning and implementation. Gradually the idea emerged of running a series of five lectures, timed to culminate on the date of Martin Luther's dramatic protestation in October 1517, on topics that could throw a contemporary light on some of the issues with which Luther was most concerned.

The five lectures, which were held at St Peter's Methodist Church in Canterbury, took place on successive Wednesday evenings from 27 September to 25 October 2017. Well-known speakers were invited to deliver the lectures, and each accepted the challenge. The programme (which could not be run in quite the intended order because of the speakers' availability) was:

God – has he changed in the 500 years since Luther?
The Reverend the Lord Griffiths
Superintendent Minister, Wesley's Chapel, London

The Bible – can it still be read as the unique truth about God?
Ms Veronica Zundel
Non-fictional writer, poet and devotional writer

Justification by Faith – what might it mean today?
Fr Tom Herbst OFM
Writer and theologian

The Creeds – is it still possible to say them without denying one's intellect?
The Reverend Professor Frances Young
Emeritus Professor of Theology, Birmingham University

Jesus – how can we understand that he is the saviour of the world?
The Right Reverend Michael Nazir-Ali
President of OXTRAD and former Bishop of Rochester

The lectures, which each attracted an attendance of about 180 people from a wide range of churches and traditions, were chaired by the Right Reverend Trevor Willmott, Bishop of Dover.

It is well-known that Martin Luther had a great love of music. He wrote that: '.... next to the Word of God, music deserves the highest praise'. You are invited to read and approach these texts of our five lectures in Canterbury, here reproduced and edited by Prof. John Butler, as though they are the score of a great 5-movement symphony. It is our hope that you will hear and catch something of the exciting demands, challenges and diverse harmonies of God's Word in today's world.

Four of the lectures have been recorded, and can be accessed at:
http://www.canterburymethodistchurch.co.uk/pod.php

1

God: has he changed in the 500 years since Luther?
by The Reverend the Lord Griffiths
Superintendent Minister, Wesley's Chapel, London

Talk given at St Peter's Methodist Church, Canterbury, 18 October 2017

Exactly fifty years ago I arrived in Cambridge to begin my studies as a Methodist minister-in-training. It so happened that Wesley House gained a new Principal at that very same time. He was Gordon Rupp, one of the finest Luther scholars in the entire world. He soon became the first non-Anglican to gain a chair in the Divinity Faculty of Cambridge University as the Dixie Professor of Ecclesiastical History. He also became my friend, and I thank God for the support and encouragement which he continued to give, especially in the difficult days we lived through at the beginning of my ministry in Haiti. Regular book parcels arrived to ensure that I remained 'a thinking and a reading man'. I greatly enjoyed what I learned about Luther in the lecture halls and from books, but I picked up just as much from the informal contacts I enjoyed with Gordon. In all these ways, I became aware that the tidal wave caused by Luther raised questions and made challenges which continue to demand action and answers down to our own day. It's with great pride that I dedicate this little excursion into the thinking of Martin Luther this evening to the memory of my beloved mentor, teacher, colleague and friend, Ernest Gordon Rupp.

For all that, I want to begin this lecture in the 17th rather than the 16th century and with my father-in-law's older brother, my wife Margaret's Uncle John! He was a serious atheist, and at the end of our first time together he thrust a slim book into my hand and urged me to read it carefully. It was a novel by Aldous Huxley entitled *Grey Eminence* and was the story of a Capuchin priest named François Leclerc du Tremblay. He was the right hand man, the grey eminence, who served as trouble shooter for Cardinal Richelieu, the power behind the throne of the young king Louis XIII. He was ruthless in directing operations on the battlefield as he hunted down Protestants on behalf of his earthly fathers, and his efforts certainly contributed to the prolonging of atrocities in the Thirty Years War. That was his day job, but at night he engaged in other activities. He composed spiritual guidance for an order of nuns in his care and wrestled in prayer for the problems of the world – all in obedience to the will of his heavenly father. The novel is an exploration of the way these two apparently contradictory sides of François Leclerc's life could be reconciled in one person.

But that wasn't Uncle John's reason for putting this novel my way. From his own reading of this lesser known of Huxley's novels, he'd become engrossed by a long excursus within the novel that describes a radical change in the nature of popular Christian devotion. This began to come about towards the end of the 14th century and spread from the Netherlands to parts of Germany, France and Italy. It laid stress on the inner life of the individual and encouraged methodical meditation especially on the life and passion of Christ. Its classic expression is to be seen in Thomas ā Kempis's *Imitation of Christ.* This approach to the spiritual life was known as the *via moderna.* St Augustine, St Bernard and St Bonaventure were among its acknowledged spiritual guides. The movement made its way among the people chiefly through free associations of secular priests and lay people, called 'Brethren of the Common Life.' It represented a radical departure from the traditional forms of the past.

A radical change in popular Christian devotion

There are two pictures that became embedded in my mind in those long-ago days in Cambridge and which have been part of my conscious life ever since. One of them I bought on our last day at Wesley House before moving to Paris and then to Haiti. It's a triptych painted by the van Eyck brothers (Hubert and Jan) for St Bavo's Cathedral in Ghent and it's part of a spectacular arrangement of panels on the main altar there. It dates from 1432 and depicts Christ the King flanked by the Virgin Mary to his right and John the Baptist to his left. It shows a heavy Byzantine influence. Christ is shown in majesty as the King of kings and the Lord of lords. He is dressed in fabulously expensive brocade. He is what Hans Küng describes as 'the bearded emperor and ruler of the world in the image forms of the imperial cult of late antiquity'.

The second picture was painted just 80 years later than the first but is startlingly different. It's part of the spectacular Isenheim altar piece, painted by Thomas Grünewald which now hangs in the *Unterlinden Museum* in Colmar, Alsace. The central figure is again Jesus, but this time he is depicted hanging from the cross. His writhing body is covered with the puss-laden sores and lesions that would have been recognised as marks of the bubonic plague. It was painted for a hospital and was no doubt intended to bring comfort to the thousands of people brought to see it, themselves victims of the plague. Here was the crucified God who'd himself plumbed the depths of human suffering. To his right is, once again, his mother; but this time, far from the aloof look she wears in the Ghent picture, she's fainting away into the arms of John the beloved disciple. On his left is the predictable figure of John the Baptist; but he's no longer wearing the tailored silk gown of a Flemish gentleman so much as a simple cloth covering his otherwise scantily dressed body. The crown that lies at the feet of Christ in the earlier picture contrasts clearly with the lamb at the feet of John. One speaks of glory and majesty, the other of suffering and sacrifice.

This has turned out to be a long introduction to a change in popular devotion that took place sometime in the second half of the 15th century.

This shift is discussed profoundly in Huxley's novel. He suggests that the devotion offered to an imperial Christ will be marked by feudal subservience and a readiness to offer gifts in homage to the kinglike figure. Or to the Vicar of Christ, who himself wore a magnificent crown and who also ruled in majesty. Once Christ is brought down from his throne, however, once he enters the school of suffering and identifies with the human lot, the focus changes. Human suffering becomes the arena for Christ's ministry: it is to be viewed as an enemy to fight, and Christ is cast as a Saviour who stands by us in our times of need. This, argues Huxley, is tantamount to legitimising suffering, as if we are to expect it as inevitable in our daily lives. From there, it's a short step to seeing war and disease, purveyors of such suffering, as enemies to be conquered or as evils to endure. For Huxley, this *via moderna*, this new kind of devotion, with its stress on the inner life of the individual, is the key to understanding the mind of François Leclerc. And, argues Huxley, it's this as much as anything that created the mind-set that underlay the readiness of Christian nations to go to war with each other down the succeeding centuries.

The world into which Martin Luther was born

It was into the midst of this cultural current, this period when one historical epoch was fading into another, that Martin Luther was born in in the year 1483. Luther's spiritual life was deeply rooted in the older traditions which honoured a Christ clothed in majesty, but his struggles led him to see Christ as a crucified God in whom and through whom a true understanding of God's justice and human salvation are to be found. The social and political turmoil unleashed by the Reformation would have offered a spectacle of Armageddon-like proportions as the unity of the Holy Roman Empire was ruptured and, out of the rubble of one political system, another was being born. Could Luther have guessed at these events? Were they unintended consequences? Were the tectonic plates buried deep in the cultural subconscious ready to crash and clash in a way that, Luther or no Luther, huge destructive energy would be released? Who can answer these questions? What is certain is that the European Union (of its day) was split in two as one Brexit moment followed another and the nation states of our continent began to be born. People could take back control of their regions and then worship God as they wished within them. Much blood was spilt during the painful birth of this brand new age.

This is what Uncle John wanted to draw to my attention. Would the worship of a suffering God in some way make us less critical of, less sensitive to, suffering in the world around us? Can that kind of devotion be seen as undergirding the ethos of a European theatre whose nations and dynasties were to turn to arms with ever greater intensity in their struggle for power and influence? Huxley very cleverly suggests that one ugly war after another, right down to the outbreak of the First World War, can be attributed to the shift in popular devotion from a majestic Christ to a suffering Jesus. Uncle John was intrigued by these possibilities. And who can doubt that they continue to haunt us down to the present time?

Martin Luther and the *via antiqua*

So let's get back to Luther and trace these matters in greater depth. In the years between his becoming a member of the Reformed Congregation of the Eremitical Order of St. Augustine in Erfurt and the pinning of the 95 theses to the cathedral doors in Wittenberg twelve years later, he seems to have emerged like an early modern butterfly from the chrysalis of the late medieval world, from the period depicted by the Van Eyck brothers, into a brand new world whose themes and ethos were so well represented by Grünewald. He seems to have attended the deathbed of one world while assisting at the birth of a new one.

Yet for all his later development, Luther's beginnings were firmly rooted in the *via antiqua,* not least through the diligent way he went about his monastic duties and followed the Rule. He was a faithful and loyal monk trained in the old ways of thinking. He was ordained priest in April 1507 after reading a treatise on the Canon of the Mass by the famous

Tübingen preacher Gabriel Biel, a work which would have led him to approach the sacred rite with an overwhelming sense of the Divine Majesty and an exalted understanding of the duty that fell up on him as one committed to intercede with the Living God. Luther was picked out for advanced training in the University of Erfurt, and it's here that we can notice his first questioning of tradition. This was occasioned by the prevalence of the thinking of Aristotle which had become an essential ingredient in the teaching of the scholastics, especially the work of Thomas Aquinas. So it seems ironical that when he was sent to teach in the recently founded University of Wittenberg in 1508, the text on which he was required to lecture was Aristotle's *Nichomachean Ethics*.

Luther and the early Wittenberg years

It was at Wittenberg that Luther met Johann von Staupitz who was to be a kind of father-in-God through his recurring times of melancholy and depression. Staupitz had studied at the universities of Cologne, Leipzig and Tübingen – all associated with the older devotional tradition. His theology was firmly Augustinian. Soon, Luther was sent back to Erfurt in the role of Sentenarius – to teach the *Sentences* of Peter of Lombard, the great theological text book of the Middle Ages. This remained a source of continuing inspiration to him throughout his life, representing as it did the twelfth century combination of Scripture and the Fathers on the eve of the invasion of Aristotle. Luther's theology was thoroughly traditional and unexceptional, centred clearly in the teaching of the Bible, Augustine and the Fathers. There are no signs yet of the revolutionary thinking that was so soon to pour out from him. He was soaked in the theology of his day, drawing sustenance from the old order even as he was becoming aware of the new ways of thinking.

At the level of church politics, too, Luther accepted the authority of Rome and paid due and filial respect to the Pope. He and a fellow monk were sent to the Eternal City in 1510. It was to be a momentous journey which played its part in introducing a deep unease into Luther's mind. As Rome came into sight Luther prostrated himself and cried out in simple piety: 'Hail, holy Rome!' But he was soon disgusted by what he found there. Gordon Rupp, in *Luther's Progress to the Diet of Worms*, painted the scene brilliantly.

> 'Despite the absence of Pope and court', he wrote, '[Luther encountered] an emotional climax of bustle, swagger and Italian panache, great buildings, churches innumerable, and acres and acres of unintelligible and reverend ruins. Luther was disgusted by the Roman clergy with their slick and cynical professionalism, as they murmured their devotions at high speed, nudging him angrily with *Passa, Passa*! Get a move on, you! … He was simple enough, and good enough, to be deeply shocked by some of the things he saw, by the living proof of the tales of vice and luxury, covetousness and degradation in high places. As he formed his impressions of the life of the church in Rome, he found himself wondering if what he had seen could possibly be true. "I would never have believed that the Papacy was such an abomination", he later wrote, "if I had not myself seen the Roman court".

Soon after his return from Rome, with prodding and encouragement from Staupitz, Luther proceeded to his doctorate, and with that came the end of his academic formation. At the age of twenty-eight, he was a Doctor of Divinity and a Professor of Sacred Theology, destined to spend the rest of his life in Wittenberg. I've wanted in these preceding paragraphs to show just how steeped Luther was in the old learning, how traditional a member of his religious order he was. He was deeply versed in the Fathers of the Church, the teaching and the Rule of his Order, and the routines of his daily life. If he favoured the teaching of Peter of Lombard above those of Thomas Aquinas, or the Bible over Aristotle, Luther was no different from so many others. He seems to have been unaffected by recent or contemporary events in other parts of Europe.

And what events they were! The whole continent was in turmoil. As Heinz Schilling has put it in *Rebellion in an Age of Upheaval*:

'The European power constellation that came into being during the first decades of Martin Luther's life was dominated by the Ottoman and Habsburg-Spanish empires, with all their alliances and rivalries, and would significantly influence the course of the Reformation. In the 1520s and 1530s the Emperor's attention was repeatedly redirected away from the Empire as he dealt not only with his kingly responsibilities within Spain but also with wars against the Turks and against his European rivals, in particular the kings of France and the pope, leaving him without the time to deal with the "Luther affair". The battles and diplomatic manoeuvres of these decades are still etched on the historical consciousness of Europe.'

Luther showed little interest in humanism – though he was certainly aware of Erasmus. Nor did he refer to the activities of Jan Huss in Bohemia or Girolamo Savonarola in Florence. There was a clearly definable groundswell of unrest at the state of the Church, but at the time he began his professorial life, Luther revealed himself as the product of the *via antiqua*. Glimpses of an independence of spirit or an energy that would focus on revival or renewal or revolution are rare to espy at this stage. So where did that burst of energy, that outburst of vehement and passionate pleading, come from? How did Luther move his understanding of God from the formulae and teaching of the schools into something altogether rawer, deeper and more personal? In a word, how did this quiet man who thought so much come to set fire to all the combustible materials that lay across the entire continent of Europe?

Luther's *Anfechtung*

I believe there are two strands to the development of Luther in the years following his appointment to Wittenberg which bear some analysis. The first springs from his personality. He seems to have had a melancholic streak and suffered from what was variously called by the spiritual directors of his age 'scruples', or 'the dark night of the soul'. And through the very same period (1511 -1521), he was wrestling with the Scriptures in a way that was to yield his new and life-changing understanding of God. So, though I must treat these two strands separately, we must make an effort to keep them very much together in our minds.

First of all, there was what must seem to modern minds a worrying obsession with death. As Luther entered the monastery, the death he stood in fear of would have been as much the one that led to judgement as to the mere cessation of life. But he was motivated by the promise of his monastic community that the possession of 'eternal life' would be a consequence of keeping the Rule. So Luther set out to secure this promise by the diligence with which he attended to the duties of the cloister. Many years later, he was to write that 'if the monastic life could get a man to heaven, I should have entered: all my companions who knew me would bear witness to that'.

Luther modelled his life on that of the desert fathers and exercised himself in austerities to the point of danger. He began well but soon felt attacked by the Devil – not with 'carnal temptations' but about deep-seated problems relating to the nature of his calling. He sought to deal with these trials through his confessions, believing that the goal of perfection required him to live faultlessly. He found that this approach to his problems withered all joy and brought him a torment of doubt and uncertainty and guilt, an inner scepticism which ate corrosively through all the offices of consolation which were offered him.

> 'My conscience could never give me certainty, but I always doubted and said, "You did not perform that correctly. You were not contrite enough. You left that out of your confession." The more I tried to remedy an uncertain, weak and afflicted conscience with the traditions of men, the more each day found it more uncertain, weaker, more troubled.'

Luther experimented with all kinds of disciplines, traditions and methods but with identical outcomes. He refused the advice of those who urged him to be kinder to himself, fearing that such advice would lead to a lack of focus, a watering down of the ideal he was seeking. He simply could not forget 'the fear of the Lord'. His word, *anfechtung,* for the obstacles which temptation put in his way reveals the way he saw his spiritual progress in terms of constant struggle.

> 'I fell away from faith and let myself think nothing less than that I had come under the Wrath of God, whom I must reconcile with my good works……[I found] God horrifyingly angry with me, with the whole creation. There can be no flight, no consolation, neither within nor without, but all is accusation. I am cast away from Thy face: Lord accuse me not in Thy Wrath. In this moment, marvellous to relate, the soul believes it can never be redeemed, but that it is suffering a punishment not yet complete….and left only with naked longing for help, and terrifying trembling, but it knows not whence help can come.'

However self-indulgent or melodramatic a modern reader might find this and other similar descriptions, it must surely impress us with its picture of utter and total despair where even one's best efforts left one worse, rather than better, placed to plead one's case before the Almighty. It was Luther's old mentor who helped him navigate these troubled waters. 'If I didn't praise Staupitz', he wrote, 'I should be a damnable, ungrateful, papistical ass….for he was my first father in this teaching, and he bore me in Christ. If he had not helped me out, I should have been swallowed up and left in hell.' Staupitz brought the wholesome corrective of the *via antiqua*, with its emphasis on the design of God and the work of grace within the human soul and, alongside that, he brought the mystical emphasis of the *via moderna* which found temptation and tribulation to be a sign of grace, a mark of conformity with Christ.

Luther and the *via moderna*

It was Staupitz who, while they were studying the Greek text of the New Testament together, helped Luther understand the authentic meaning of 'penitence' as 'repent' rather than 'do penance'. 'This word of yours', he wrote to Staupitz, 'stuck in me like "a sharp arrow of the mighty" (Psalm 120:4)'. But his doubts were not yet over: the idea of predestination (so clearly present in all the text books) led him to writhe in anguish lest he should never be worthy of finding himself among the elect. On good days, he felt tempted by the fact that there seemed no temptations to worry him! But all in all, we can see how, at every turn, Luther felt his attempts, following scholastic teaching, to make acts of love to God were choked off, resulting in a constrained and hypocritical devotion, while deep down he felt a murmuring against a God who weighted everything against the sinner, driving him almost to the point of explicit and open blasphemy.

So much for Luther's psychological struggles alongside which (and interpenetrated by which) we must now take a moment to consider his Biblical studies. Across these critical first years of his public ministry, he delivered courses of lectures which show his deep knowledge of the scriptures and also the emergence of his spiritual awakening. The courses were on the Psalms in 1513-1514; Romans in 1515-1516; Galatians in 1516-1517; Hebrews in 1517-1518; and the Psalms once again in 1519. Günther Bornkamm put these studies very succinctly into their proper context: 'One thing is clear – the inmost, most personal experience of Luther, and his scholarly, theological, above all exegetical discoveries cannot be separated; the secret lies in the indissoluble unity of personal experience and theological and exegetical research.' Or, as Luther himself put it, 'I did not learn my theology all at once, but I had to search deeper for it, where my temptations took me'.

These lectures show Luther distancing himself from the Aristotelian idea of the soul and also the neo-Platonic division between soul and body. He begins to form a new anthropology of the whole person, the conception of a human being confronted in all their personal existence by the person of the living God. He still clings to much of the teaching of St. Augustine but reaches and teaches a more radical diagnosis of human sin which, he argues, resides in our egoism. Concupiscence, such a large theme for Augustine, is no longer conceived by Luther as merely the desire of the flesh; inbred (original) sin is to be understood as a restless self-regard active and working even in our dreams. The inspiration of the Holy Spirit alone can help us address this state of affairs. It becomes urgent for men and women to find a righteousness which comes from without. We cannot be released from the state we're in by any attributes or energies that are born within us. And God alone is the giver of that gift. It is not, definitely not, the imputation of the merits of Christ, a piece of celestial electronic banking with credit transferred from God's account to ours. It is nothing less than the living Christ in his own person filling us with his presence.

This faith is not an intellectual acceptance of a new truth but a new experience of an old and timeless truth that is to be believed and known in all its glory. Romans 8:26 shows that the Spirit of God is no longer a transcendent cause of salvation but the living personal presence of God, at work, and interceding for us with groans that cannot be uttered. This, according to Luther, is a realisation that can be accepted with gladness, willingness and spontaneity by all those who love the will of God. It is from this starting point, as Luther himself put it, that believers can grow 'from good to better as a sick man moves from sickness to health'. It shows God as the Good Samaritan who finds the sinner half dead but takes him into his care until he is cured.

On the question of predestination which had so sorely tested him psychologically, Luther offers poignant and kindly wisdom. We might well throw our hands in the air in horror as we speculate whether we're among the chosen or not. But once we meditate the wounds of Christ, we might well find ourselves faced by a radical question. Did he really go through all that simply to offer grace to a chosen few? We should be kind to ourselves just as God is kind to us and believe that what God has done for us in Christ will feed and nurture us, build and bolster us, hold and heal us. He anticipated the thinking of Isaac Watts who, two centuries later, was to write about the 'wondrous cross' where 'sorrow and love flow mingled down' - words which generate the burning question that still engenders hope for any beleaguered soul: 'Did e'er such love and sorrow meet or thorns compose so rich a crown?'

Luther's significant turning point

All of this was going on in Luther's head and heart before the Church controversy that began in 1517. But it was in 1519, while lecturing for a second time on the Psalms, that a very significant turning point came to him.

> 'I turned once more to interpret the Psalms, relying on the fact that I was the more expert after I had handled in the schools the letters of St Paul to the Romans and Galatians, and that which is to the Hebrews … It was not coldness of blood which held me up but this one word that is in Romans Chapter 1. The Justice of God, which by the use and custom of all doctors I had been taught to understand philosophically as they say, as that formal and active justice whereby God is just and punishes unjust sinners.

> 'For, however irreproachable my life as a monk, I felt myself, in the presence of God, to be a sinner with a most unquiet conscience, nor would I believe him to be pleased with my satisfaction. I did not love, indeed I hated this just God who punished sinners, and if not with silent blasphemy, at least with huge murmuring, I was indignant against God, as if it were really not enough that miserable sinners, eternally ruined by original sin, should be crushed with every kind of calamity by the law of the Ten Commandments, but God through the Gospel must add sorrow on sorrow, and through the Gospel bring his wrath and justice to bear on us. I raged with a fierce and disturbed conscience in this way, and yet I knocked with importunity at Paul in this place with a burning desire to know what St Paul could intend.

> 'At last, God being merciful, as I meditated day and night, pondering the connection of the words, namely "The Justice of God is revealed, as it is written, The Just shall live by faith", there I began to understand that Justice of God in which the just man

lives by the gift of God, i.e. by faith, and this sentence, "the Justice of God is revealed in the Gospel" to be understood passively as that whereby the merciful God justifies us by faith, as it is written, "the just shall live by faith". At this I felt myself to be born anew, and to enter through open gates into paradise itself. From here, the whole face of the Scriptures was altered. I ran through the Scriptures as memory served, and collected the same analogy in other words as *opus dei*, that which God works in us; *virtus dei*, that in which God makes us strong; *sapientia dei*, in which he makes us wise; *fortitudo dei, salus dei, gloria dei*.

'And now, as much as I formerly hated the words "Justice of God" so now did I love and extol it as the sweetest of all words and then this solace was to me as the gates of paradise. Afterwards, I read St. Augustine, "Of the Spirit and the Letter", and beyond all hope, found that he also similarly interpreted the Justice of God as that with which God clothes us and by which we are justified: .... armed with these cogitations I began the second course on the Psalms ...'

Scholarly perspectives

I began by describing two modes of devotion shown in the iconography of the 14th and 15th centuries. As I conclude, let me ask you to look again at those pictures as I quote three scholars who try to sum up the ground and the issues I've been trying to explore with you. Here are the Van Eyck brothers and Grünewald in words rather than pictures.

First Gordon Rupp (*Luther's Progress to the Diet of Worms*): Luther made a clear distinction between a 'Theology of the Cross' rooted in Christ crucified and revealing a true knowledge of God and a 'Theology of Glory', a theology of speculation on the attributes of deity which is ignorant that 'God is not found save in sufferings and in the Cross'.

And then Heinz Schilling (*Rebellion in an Age of Upheaval*): Luther's experience prepared the way for a paradigm shift in the anthropology of devotion that would have profound historical consequences, as the performance-based medieval understanding of piety was replaced by the grace-focused piety of early modern Protestantism.

And finally, Karl Holl (*The Reconstruction of Morality*): The word 'Justitia' lay in tension between two mighty vocabularies – the Hellenic concept of Justice and the Biblical theme of the Righteousness of God. This had long been a problem for Luther; he saw it as the hammer of God's wrath which he uses on all of us, sinners as we all are. But he came to see it all so differently. As Holl put it: 'The illumination came when, through this very concept "Justice", there burst the saving intervention of a merciful God, displayed in Jesus Christ and freely bestowed on sinners. God does not send His Grace alongside His Righteousness, but He sends it through His Righteousness … This was more than a new exposition of Romans 1:17….it was the fountain spring of a new doctrine of God.'

Postscript: I got carried away once I'd begun writing this lecture. I was asked to explore the way Luther's doctrine of God continued to resonate down the ages. I had every intention of offering cameo considerations of three recent theologians, all German by origin, namely Dietrich Bonhoeffer, Reinhold Niebuhr and Jürgen Moltmann, to show how Luther's theology had underpinned their thinking and given strength to the causes they advocated. And I also wanted to put Luther's contribution to modern theological understanding up against what we might call 'neo-Calvinism' in order to show a warmer, more generous, altogether more optimistic understanding of grace. But time ran out as would your patience if I'd stuck to my original intentions.

2

The Bible: Can it still be read as the unique truth about God?
by Ms Veronica Zundel
Non-fictional writer, poet and devotional writer

Talk given at St Peter's Methodist Church, Canterbury, 4 October 2017

To begin with a disclaimer: I have very little formal theological education, though I have a lifelong interest in theology and I have been writing daily Bible notes for over 35 years, as well as a period spent editing them. As an English literature graduate, I tend to approach the Bible from a literary or narrative viewpoint, which leads me to see it much more as a collection of powerful stories than as a propositional document which has to be decoded into a set of abstract principles. I've also spent 24 years as an active member of a Mennonite church and a regular preacher there, which gives me a somewhat different perspective on the Reformation, not least because the Mennonites belong to a tradition - the Anabaptist tradition - that has been persecuted by both Catholics and Protestants!

The title for this evening's talk is 'The Bible: Can it still be read as the unique truth about God?' I'd like to approach the question by examining the *second* most important three-letter word in the English Bible. You might guess that the *most* important three-letter word is 'God'. I want to suggest that the second most important is 'but'. And specifically, the 'but' that appears in these verses which open the book of Hebrews:

> 'Long ago God spoke to our ancestors in many and various ways by the prophets, *but* in these last days he has spoken to us by a Son, whom he appointed heir of all things, through whom he also created the worlds. He is the reflection of God's glory and the exact imprint of God's very being, and he sustains all things by his powerful word.' (Hebrews 1:1-3a)

Why does verse 2 begin with the word 'but' and not the word 'and'? Surely, if Jesus, among his many other roles, is the greatest of the prophets, and has come, in his own words, to fulfil the law, this verse should read: 'God spoke to our ancestors ... by the prophets, *and* in these last days he has spoken to us by a Son'? But no: the writer of Hebrews deliberately chooses the word 'but', which implies a certain discontinuity as well as a connection. And while I cannot say that Anabaptists use this passage to justify their particular approach to the Bible, I do think it encapsulates their hermeneutic, or principle of interpretation, which is very different from that of the mainstream Reformers. I want to look at three aspects of that Anabaptist hermeneutic in the hope that it may throw some light on the wider implications of the question facing me tonight.

A Jesus-centred hermeneutic

Firstly, from the point of view of an Anabaptist interpretation, the use of this little word 'but' relativizes everything that goes before it. The Bible can no longer be seen as a uniform document in which every part is equally relevant - or, as 2 Timothy 3:16 puts it, 'useful'. 'But' implies that there is something greater here, in which God speaks to us by a Son. The former communications or revelations were partial and incomplete; they were pieces of the picture of God but not the whole picture.

I don't mean to imply by this that the rest of the Bible becomes less important. I don't even mean it becomes less authoritative, although the nature of its authority may change. What I do mean is that no part of the Bible can now be read independently of God's revelation in Jesus. Everything now has to be related to Jesus. And for the Anabaptist tradition, this means that it has to be read in the light of his life and teaching as well as in the light of his death and resurrection.

This 'Jesus-centred hermeneutic' overcomes what the scholar and liturgist Eleanor Kreider - one of the founders of my Mennonite congregation - calls 'the Jesus-shaped hole' in our classic Christian creeds. Have you ever noticed how all the historic creeds go straight from 'born of the virgin Mary' to 'suffered under Pontius Pilate' with nothing in between: no teaching, no ministry, no calling of a community of disciples, in fact practically no Jesus except the one who came to die for our sins and rise again? I accept that the creeds were formulated to address historic doctrinal controversies around the meaning of salvation and the nature of God. Nevertheless, this is a curiously Jesus-free version of faith, and by focusing, as Luther did, on the role of the cross in determining our eternal destiny, it ends up with little to say about how we should be living in *this* world.

In contrast, the Anabaptist hermeneutic places Jesus, including his earthly life, at the centre of biblical interpretation and hence at the centre of understanding how we are to live in this world. Jesus is the hermeneutical key to the rest of the scriptures, and this means not just searching for hints and premonitions of Christ in the Old Testament but refusing to read any other part of the Bible except through the lens of Jesus. Thus, the rest of the Bible has value as 'rules to live by' or as 'guidance on how to run a life or a society' *only* to the extent that we can reinterpret it in the light of Jesus.

This has not only theological and ecclesiological implications but huge political ones as well. Sometimes known as 'the radical reformation', the Anabaptists' disagreement with the magisterial reformers centred around a number of things, both in church polity and in the relationship of the church to the society around it. Essentially, the mainstream reformers accepted the continuation of a geographical, rather than a discipleship, model of faith and church. That is to say, if you were born into a Christian country or region you were automatically a Christian and you were initiated into the church from birth. What had been automatically Catholic areas simply became automatically Lutheran or Calvinist areas. This inevitably implied that Christians had a privileged status in relation to the governance of an area: it was meant to be run on Christian principles, usually to the disadvantage of anyone who did not identify as a Christian. We know, for example, how negatively Luther felt towards the Jews – something that I, as a Jew by birth, feel strongly about.

In relation to the Bible, the reformers - who could be seen as the precursors of modern individualism - essentially identified the New Testament as being about individual salvation. This was, and still is for most churches, focused on a future heaven. It does, of course, have implications for how we should live in *this* world, but these implications are mostly about personal morality and integrity. As a result, the reformers were left with no model of how to run a 'Christian' society except the theocracy, or perhaps the would-be theocracy, of the Old Testament, with all its panoply of enforced conformity to the law of God and the use of violence to back it up. Hence the reformers, just like the Catholic tradition they were supposedly reforming, continued to hunt heresy or misbehaviour and to punish or attempt to expunge it with what Anabaptists called 'the sword' but which might equally be the stake and the bonfire.

From an Anabaptist viewpoint, this approach failed to engage with the teachings of Christ, especially his teachings about non-violence and non-retaliation. To the Anabaptists, the use of violence to impose conformity was at odds with what they called 'the perfection of Christ'. Since the societies in which they lived had grown habituated to such violence, it meant that those who wanted to live by a different standard would have to form alternative communities in which forgiveness and reconciliation could be practised as Jesus had taught. This also chimed in with their understanding of the church as a community of professed disciples - a 'believers' church'- that had no earthly power but that lived in the power of the Holy Spirit.

A progressive view of scripture

That little phrase 'the perfection of Christ' leads me to my second observation about an Anabaptist view of scripture, and again it is encapsulated in the opening verses of Hebrews and in that little word 'but'. It is that the Anabaptists had a progressive view of revelation centuries before such a thing became fashionable. Here we have to look to another passage where that little word 'but' features prominently: the Sermon on the Mount. I'll read excerpts from Matthew 5:21 onwards:

'You have heard that it was said to those of ancient times, "You shall not murder"; and "whoever murders shall be liable to judgment". *But* I say to you that if you are angry with a brother or sister, you will be liable to judgment; and if you insult a brother or sister, you will be liable to the council; and if you say, "You fool", you will be liable to the hell of fire…

You have heard that it was said, "You shall not commit adultery". *But* I say to you that everyone who looks at a woman with lust has already committed adultery with her in his heart…

It was also said, "Whoever divorces his wife, let him give her a certificate of divorce". *But* I say to you that anyone who divorces his wife, except on the ground of unchastity, causes her to commit adultery; and whoever marries a divorced woman commits adultery…

Again, you have heard that it was said to those of ancient times, "You shall not swear falsely, but carry out the vows you have made to the Lord". *But* I say to you, do not swear at all… Let your word be "Yes, Yes" or "No, No"; anything more than this comes from the evil one…

You have heard that it was said, "An eye for an eye and a tooth for a tooth". *But* I say to you, do not resist an evildoer. *But* if anyone strikes you on the right cheek, turn the other also; and if anyone wants to sue you and take your coat, give your cloak as well; and if anyone forces you to go one mile, go also the second mile…

You have heard that it was said, "You shall love your neighbour and hate your enemy". *But* I say to you, love your enemies and pray for those who persecute you, so that you may be children of your Father in heaven; for he makes his sun rise on the evil and on the good, and sends rain on the righteous and on the unrighteous.

'*But* in these last days he has spoken by a Son'. '*But* I say unto you'. Do you see a pattern here? The revelation in Jesus, both in his teaching and in his practice, and ultimately in his crucifixion and resurrection, goes well beyond any previous revelation, and in a sense is so bright a light that anything that precedes it comes to look like shadow. Previous revelation is partial, as though seeing God in a glass darkly; the light has been gradually dawning, and now in Jesus the full light of the sun is visible.

Now at one level this is nothing new. We know this and we have been taught it: the prophets and the law give us hints and shadows, but the full revelation is in Christ, who is 'the exact imprint of God's very being' (Hebrews 1:3). What the early Anabaptists contended - and what I believe - is that we have failed to explore the full implications of this, both in how we read the Bible and how we consequentially live. And this impacts both our personal journeys of discipleship and our engagement in society.

Exploring the full implications of God's revelation is, of course, exactly what Jesus himself is doing in the extracts we read from the Sermon on the Mount. He is taking the injunctions of the Hebrew Scriptures and remodelling them in the light of his own choice of non-violence and unconditional love. He is not discarding the provisions of the Jewish law – after all, he was a Jew himself – but he *is* exposing their ultimate inadequacy and partiality, and in so doing he is proposing what Paul might call 'a more excellent way'.

Take for instance 'an eye for an eye, a tooth for a tooth'. In its original context it was less a statutory sentencing policy than an ordinance of limitation: in order to avoid an escalation of violence, you were not to take more in return than had been taken by the offender. In Jesus this is taken still further through its transformation into the law of love: you don't take even an eye or a tooth, but rather you seek reconciliation through the way of forgiveness and acceptance. This is the true meaning of Jesus 'fulfilling the law': that he takes the Old Testament provision for a spiritually healthy life and society and he moves it towards its logical conclusion, in what the New Testament calls 'the law of Christ'.

In the Sermon on the Mount, Jesus is offering us not only a radical way to live as individuals in society, but also a powerful model of how to read the Jewish scriptures in the light of the new covenant he is initiating. I'm surprised that this has so rarely been noticed or commented on. Perhaps we prefer the simple straightforward rule-based policies of the Old Testament to the creative, risky strategies that Jesus proposes and that his disciples follow in the New Testament? I think there is a great deal of work yet to be done exploring the imaginative and frankly sometimes cavalier way that New Testament writers, and Jesus himself, re-apply the Jewish scriptures in their teaching.

It is interesting that there have been numerous attempts by earnest Christians to call society back to the values of the Ten Commandments, which of course are Jewish, not Christian; but I can think of no movements to recall society back to the Sermon on the Mount – perhaps because we've rarely attempted to follow it in the first place. I think it was G K Chesterton who remarked that Christianity had not been tried and found wanting, rather it had been found difficult and not tried.

Diverse voices in scripture

The third aspect I want to draw out from the opening of Hebrews (and this is less directly relatable to an Anabaptist hermeneutic and history) is the recognition that there are diverse voices in scripture – summed up in that little phrase 'many and various ways'. Hebrews recognizes that the Jewish scriptures do not speak with a single voice or offer a single version of either theology or salvation history.

This is easily demonstrated by looking at the different views of kingship in the Old Testament. When, for instance, in 1 Samuel 8, the people asked Yahweh to appoint 'a king like other nations', Samuel gave an unrelentingly negative view of what a king would do: he would recruit the nation's sons to his army and exploit its daughters to service the needs of his court. By contrast, the books of Kings and Chronicles have a more ambivalent view of kingship, listing kings who did right in the sight of the Lord and kings who did evil. Yet still preachers and teachers insist on peddling 'what the Bible teaches' about X or Y, failing to recognize the varying viewpoints from which we have to synthesise a Christian attitude.

Oddly enough, 'what the Bible teaches' seems to be far more common than 'what Jesus teaches' - perhaps another instance of the Jesus-shaped hole in our theology, a hole that has been filled by elevating the Bible to practically the fourth member of the Trinity. This is perhaps where the idea of diverse voices connects with an Anabaptist hermeneutic: what we ultimately need to do is to subject the varying voices of the Bible, including the apparently conflicting voices in the New Testament, to the test of how they compare to the teaching of Jesus.

This seems to me to be what Luther so egregiously failed to do when he dismissed the epistle of James – a book beloved of Mennonites and other Anabaptists – as an 'epistle of straw'. Having established 'justification by faith' as his yardstick for evaluating and interpreting scripture, he then measured the epistle of James against this yardstick and found it wanting. But was this the right yardstick in the first place? What if, instead, Luther had taken this epistle traditionally attributed to Jesus' own brother and measured it by the yardstick of Jesus' own teaching? I suspect he would then have found it a deeply 'Jesus-flavoured' epistle, which does not fall into thinking we can be saved by works, but instead insists that the faith which opens us to salvation by grace is not a true faith unless it issues in works. In other words, we are not saved *by* good works but we are absolutely saved *for* good works.

The voice of James, different from the voice of Paul, then becomes an essential corrective to the seeds of antinomianism that Paul warns against in Romans 6:1-2: 'What then are we to say? Should we continue in sin in order that grace may abound? By no means! How can we who died to sin go on living in it?'

While we are looking at Romans, I want to share something I only discovered after nearly forty years of being a Christian: that up to the Reformation, the phrase rendered in verses such as Romans 3:22 as 'faith *in* Jesus Christ', was normally translated as 'the faith (or the faithfulness) *of* Jesus Christ'. If this is true, then it gives us a significantly different emphasis from Luther's interpretation. It suggests that we are not saved by our own faith, which can so easily be turned into another kind of work, but by the faith exercised by Jesus as he lived a life and died a death characterized by trust in and obedience to God. Even our translations, then, can reveal a bias which is not necessarily true to the Bible but is deformed by our own theological preconceptions. I can't believe that no one ever told me this in all those years – as if there is a conspiracy to put forward an essentially Lutheran interpretation and no other.

There is another aspect of recognizing diversity in the Bible, which connects more immediately with my Anabaptist tradition: the need for a diversity of voices to *interpret* it. The early Anabaptists insisted that the scriptures were to be interpreted within the discipleship community; they were not to be limited to ready-made interpretations handed down from above. This goes with their view that the Holy Spirit, who leads us into all truth, is given to the gathered community as a whole, *not* to specially gifted individuals. This is not to encourage what has sometimes been called 'the sharing of ignorance', or to deny the role of scholars and the theologically educated. Indeed, the early Anabaptists had many highly trained scholars amongst them and made use of their insights. But it is to say that anyone who talks about God from a position of commitment to Jesus is a theologian whose voice has a right to be heard.

This favouring of communal interpretation also reflects the Anabaptist view of the church as a distinctive *community*, not as an authoritative *institution*. Which is perhaps where I should introduce you to 'Zundel's law of community', which defines the difference between a community and an institution thus: 'when people join an institution, they have to change to fit the institution, but when they join a community, both they and the community change'. But that could be a whole separate talk.

A canon within the canon?

I talked earlier of Luther's choice of yardstick for evaluating the epistle of James. A theological term for a yardstick is of course a 'canon'; and this brings me to one of the objections to an Anabaptist hermeneutic: that it creates a canon within a canon, or more negatively, a pick and mix approach to the Bible. In reality, we all have our own 'canon within the canon' whereby we privilege certain parts of scripture over others, or we use them as a lens with which to view others. There is not necessarily anything wrong with this. For instance, no one except the Seventh Day Adventists believes we are obliged to keep all the Jewish food laws, while no one except the tiny surviving group of Samaritans still practises animal sacrifice. We have decided, on perfectly good biblical grounds, that while the Jewish moral law, in the form of the Ten Commandments, may still apply to us, the ceremonial and ritual law does not.

My problem comes when our 'canon within the canon' (by, for instance focusing on the epistles at the cost of the gospels) excludes the human life of Jesus and treats his earthly ministry merely as a route to the atonement, devoid of any moral or theological value in its own right. I have even heard the Sermon on the Mount interpreted as a demonstration of how unable we are to obey God's law in our own strength, effectively showing us how impossible it is to follow Jesus' teaching. This strikes me as a peculiar form of heresy.

Many Anabaptists would openly admit to using a 'canon within the canon': for them, the New Testament is the canon within the Bible, the gospels are the canon within the New Testament, and the Sermon on the Mount is the canon within the gospels –a canon within a canon within a canon! Whatever the faults and limitations of this may be, it does at least have the virtue of placing Jesus and his radical life and teaching at the very centre of faith. It seems to me a good measure to use in assessing how far our teaching fosters discipleship and enables us to become more

Christ-like, rather than simply more conformist to a rule-based moral code.

Speaking now from personal experience, my sense within evangelical churches in the past has been that discipleship, if it was mentioned at all, was seen predominantly in terms of avoiding a range of blatant sins – in other words, keeping our noses clean and behaving ourselves. It certainly didn't include anything that could get us killed, at least in the West, which is what I understand Jesus meant by 'taking up our cross' – that is to say, acting in a way which could lead to punishment or death at the hands of the authorities. In my Mennonite experience, I have discovered what I think I always half-knew, that discipleship is about learning to love sacrificially and riskily as Jesus loved, rather than sacrificing others on the altar of our own moral judgement.

The Jesus-centred hermeneutic in practice: genocide in the Old Testament

I'd like to finish by offering some examples of how I think a Jesus-centred hermeneutic, which acknowledges the progressive nature of revelation and the diversity of biblical voices, can be applied both to Old and New Testament interpretation.

I'd first like to look at the apparently God-ordained violence - even genocide - in the Old Testament, which causes problems not only for pacifist Anabaptists but for many others committed to non-violence. When examining such narratives, a Jesus-centred hermeneutic must put at its centre the teaching of Jesus on non-violence and non-retaliation – a teaching that led him to choose the cross rather than call down twenty legions of angels to defend him.

Starting from this foundation, Millard Lind in his book *Yahweh is a Warrior* observes that in the book of Joshua and elsewhere in the Old Testament, Israel is repeatedly told by God to limit their military strength, to eschew warhorses and chariots (which were the tanks of their day) and to go into battle significantly weaker, in military terms, than their opponents. This is so that God, rather than the Israelites themselves, can be seen to be the victor against the Canaanite forces. There is much to be said for this approach, but my problem is that it leaves us with a God who commits genocide himself rather than instructing a people to do it for him, which doesn't really help us that much.

Of course, we now know from the archaeological evidence that the book of Joshua is more an expression of aspiration than a record of history: the conquest of Canaan was far more limited and incomplete than the book of Joshua states. But this still leaves us with a people who would have liked to wipe out the inhabitants of the land, even if they didn't succeed. I find this dilemma is better addressed by a progressive view of revelation, where Joshua expresses an earlier understanding of God and his wishes that is superseded by the later non-violence of Jesus. The main point here is that these passages cannot be taken as prescriptive in any independent way – they are not even necessarily descriptive – and can only be read against the measure of the Jesus way.

The Jesus-centred hermeneutic in practice: shunning in the Mennonite tradition

This way of reading does more than help us with the problematic parts of the Old Testament. I'd like to try it on a passage which I think has actually been greatly misinterpreted by Anabaptists throughout their history. It is Matthew 18:15-20, the passage on church discipline that some scholars find so difficult that they see it as an interpolation in Jesus' teaching by a later hand. Anabaptists have traditionally understood these verses as a justification for the practice of shunning - that is, the exclusion and excommunication of church members who persists in sin despite a graded process of trying to challenge and reintegrate them.

Shunning has been much abused down the years as a way of imposing doctrinal or behavioural conformity. What can be said in its favour is that at least the Anabaptists took church discipline seriously in their quest to create a distinctive and holy Christian community; and their version of church discipline was and is a non-violent one, as opposed to earlier and more mainstream churches who imposed discipline by use of the rack and the stake. With the exception of the revolution in Münster, which was an aberration, Anabaptists have never killed anyone for their faith or lack of it.

So I appreciate that shunning was a way of keeping the community of believers distinctive and preventing them from losing their edge and witness. But (that word again!) from a truly Jesus-centred perspective I would suggest a totally opposite interpretation of these verses to the traditional one. I would focus on that last injunction to treat the unrepentant sinner 'as a Gentile and a tax collector'. If we look at Jesus' actual practice, how did he treat Gentiles and tax collectors? He called them, invited them, witnessed to them, healed them. In other words, if someone in your fellowship is not behaving as a Christian, you have to assume they are not really a Christian, and you have to witness to them. This also locates the passage much better within its biblical context, coming as it does between the parable of the lost sheep and the instruction to forgive seventy times seven.

Shunning is the practice of what mathematicians call a 'bounded set', where the divide between the Christian community and the rest of the world is clearly and firmly defined. In contrast, I think the inclusive practice of Jesus shows a 'centred set', in which the core is clearly distinguished but can afford to be fuzzy at the edges. Jesus had a committed core of disciples, certainly, but he was open to a much wider and less committed body of followers who always had the option of making – or not making - the ultimate commitment. My own Mennonite church started as a bounded set, with a novice membership scheme designed to introduce prospective members to the ethos of the church; but it moved later towards a more centred set with a small core of members whilst remaining very open to those not ready for that kind of commitment.

Can the Bible still be read as the unique truth about God?

I hope this has illustrated briefly how a Jesus-centred way of interpretation might work in practice, taking scripture seriously but recognizing that under the New Covenant in Christ its meaning and application might have changed radically from its original context. So how do we then answer that question posed in the title of this talk: 'Can the Bible still be read as the unique truth about God?' I would want to argue that it can, but that both the Bible and the truth are more complex than we often want to acknowledge. Apart from anything else, we have to remember that up to three quarters of the Bible was not written by Christians!

For me, the Bible is not a document, or even a collection of documents, that can be read in a uniform way, as a sort of engineering manual offering us a guide to life rather than to our brand of car. It never was that. It is a corporate, diverse witness that has to be interpreted corporately by a diverse community. Moreover, the Bible's own witness is that it is Jesus, rather than itself, that is the unique truth about God. 'In the beginning was the Word, and the Word was with God, and the Word was God'. This does not refer to the written word or even to the orally transmitted text, but to the one who is its inspiration, its fulfilment and its endpoint. Or as the early Anabaptist scholar Hans Denck put it, 'I hold Holy Scripture above all human treasure but not so highly as the Word of God'.

3

Justification by faith: What might it mean today?
by Father Tom Herbst OFM
Writer and theologian

Talk given at St Peter's Methodist Church, Canterbury, 11 October 2017

The question of justification is central to the Christian faith because it describes the process of salvation. As such, there is hardly any area of Christian speculative theology or doctrine that is not affected by it. Indeed, one could say (as Martin Luther certainly implied) that any theological endeavour that does not address the central and over-riding concern of justification is of little use and could even be perceived as false or obstructive. This perception can, perhaps, also be understood as the first in a set of unifying principles, since other Reformers - as well as Catholics - who may have disagreed with Luther about a host of issues, would concur with one another regarding the importance and centrality of human justification as a necessity of salvation. It is ironic that the very importance of this shared, inter-denominational perception about justification and salvation has become the cause of passionate debate covering a host of related subjects and has been used as the primary reason for the division of Western Christendom.

Justification in historical perspective

The historical inception of that story of interaction and challenge, which initiated the movement known as the Reformation almost exactly five hundred years ago, is well known. Suffice it here briefly to review the issues, as they arose in the experience of the Augustinian monk, Martin Luther, in order to establish a concrete context for what was to become a long and highly complex process of discernment, dogmatic speculation and even proclamation. It is a process that has endured right up to modern times. In his fourth volume dealing with the history of the Church, titled *The Protestant Reformation*, the French Catholic writer,

Henri Daniel-Rops made the astounding assertion that the historical sale of indulgences had a positive and salutary effect throughout late-medieval Christendom. This beneficial effect, he claimed, was manifest not only in a material way (for example the finances acquired in order literally to rebuild the French Church in the aftermath of the Hundred Years War) but also in a spiritual way, for the disposition of a penitent would *already* have been orientated to a 'state of grace', linked to reception of the Sacrament of Penance, before the indulgence was even purchased.

However much astonishment this assertion may invoke in a modern believer, whether Catholic or Protestant, Daniel-Rops's insight is valuable in reflecting attitudes that were still prevalent in the early modern world of Martin Luther. It is also important to acknowledge that Daniel-Rops immediately proceeded to list the rather crude abuses associated with the practice of selling indulgences in the early-sixteenth century Church, as well as the theology justifying such action. He specifically cited the Saxon German purview of the hapless Dominican 'salesman' Johann Tetzel. The resulting protest reached the public stage on October 31st 1517 when Martin Luther - a university professor, ordained priest, and highly regarded member of the Augustinian Order - nailed his ninety-five theses to the door of the chapel at the Castle in Wittenberg, thereby triggering the movement known as the Reformation. He was thirty-four years old.

Justification in the ninety-five theses

It is significant to note that, although many perceived abuses and errors of the Church were listed in the ninety-five theses, the assertion of justification *by faith in Christ alone* was dominant, representing the summation of Luther's arguments. Even so, as important as the catalytic issue of the sale of indulgences was to the formation of Luther's initial protest and to the articulation of his doctrine of justification by faith, it has often been noted that his psychological and spiritual disposition affected him far more profoundly. The two, of course, may not have been unrelated, and much discussion has taken place over the centuries as to what that relationship might have been. Suffice it to say here that Luther attests that his perception of Christ before his experience of 'enlightenment' (probably sometime in the years 1514 to 1518), was as a 'hangman' and his spiritual disposition was one of desolation and despair.

The substance of the 'enlightenment' experienced by Luther was based on readings in Romans 1:17 and 3:21-31, which would serve as a scriptural foundation for subsequent Protestant assertions of the many ramifications of what justification by faith (alone) might mean. This was, of course, to have a profound effect on nearly every aspect of interior and exterior Christian belief and practice, and it was in turn to form the basis for the emergence of many denominations within the Western Church; a process that continues to this day.

For Martin Luther, it is clear that the passages he discovered in Romans 1:17 and 3:21ff served as a kind of antidote to the view of God that equated him with the sweet consolation of divine mercy. This quality of 'mercy' was understood to be *complete*, in the sense of fully justifying a believing sinner; to be a *pure gift*, in the sense of proceeding solely by God's grace; and, thus, necessarily to be *wholly vicarious*. As a corollary to this view, the agency of human will was, with respect to justification, entirely nullified, thus effecting a radical separation between faith in the freely given saving power of God on the one hand and, on the other, human works that were understood to be wholly inadequate and unable to contribute to that process.

The Catholic response: *Exsurge Domine* and the Council of Trent

The Catholic response to Lutheran and other denominational views about the nature of justification, particularly its relation to human will and agency, was swift, and it found a response at the highest levels of magisterial authority. A polemic was established within the fractured fabric of Western Christendom that persists to this day and has a direct relevance to the question implied by the title of this paper: what might various understandings of justification by faith mean today? Leaving that aside for the moment, it is important first of all briefly to examine the position of the sixteenth-century Catholic Church. Two sources will suffice here.

In his 1520 Bull, *Exsurge Domine,* promulgated against errors perceived in Luther's understanding of divine grace, human will and justification by faith, Pope Leo X listed several objections that shed light on the Catholic position at the time. The necessity of good works as visible manifestations of justification was affirmed, as also was the created grace mediated by the sacraments, especially baptism; and therefore as a result of *both* works and grace, human will is engaged, for better or worse, in a partnership with the Holy Spirit in the economy of salvation.

It was not, however, until the convocation of the sixth session of the Ecumenical Council held at Trent in 1547 that the Catholic Church was able fully to articulate its position on justification by faith in response to what was perceived as the Protestant challenge. Several significant aspects of that position should be noted. First, justification, which begins and ends with faith, was understood within a three-fold, somewhat chronological, sequence: the moment when justification is attained; the beginning of its subsequent preservation and increase; and the moment of its recovery after having been lost by sin. Faith functions differently in each of these three phases of the process of justification, but it is in the second and third phases that faith is *particularly* aided by grace and mediated by a sacrament which, in turn, is mediated by the Church.

Significantly, the first chapter of the Council of Trent's decree concurs with the spirit of Luther's insight that humanity, by its own efforts – whether of reason or will - is unable to justify itself. This is followed in chapter two with the assertion that justification is only available through the expiatory grace of Christ, received by faith (with an explicit reference to Romans 3:25). This expiatory grace of redemption and justification is offered to the whole world. Yet in chapter three of the decree the effect of that justifying grace is only received by those who are 'reborn in Christ'; and this is clarified in chapter four as participation in the sacrament of baptism.

Does this imply faith? Yes, but only by implication, for the word itself is not used. Chapter five is of great significance: baptized adults have been justified by 'a predisposing grace of God through Jesus Christ ... with no existing merits of their own'. It is because of that justification that they are 'disposed by God's grace, inciting and helping them, to turn toward their own justification by giving free assent to, and cooperating with, this grace'. The door is thus left open to the efficacy of works - not when justification is bestowed in the first place but in the subsequent process of conversion.

A fruit of the initial justification brought about through faith would also correspond to the insight treasured by Luther, namely, that once a believer is justified, he or she would turn 'from fear of divine justice, which profitably strikes them, to thoughts of God's mercy'. Differences between Catholic perceptions and those of Luther and the other Reformers do, however, emerge explicitly in chapters eight and nine:

> '(VIII) When the Apostle says that a person is justified by faith and as a gift, those words are to be understood in the sense which the perennial consent of the catholic church has maintained and expressed, namely that we are said to be justified by faith because faith is the first stage of human salvation, the foundation and root of all justification without which it is *impossible to please God* and come to the fellowship of his children. And we are said to receive justification as a free gift because nothing that precedes justification, neither faith nor works, would merit the grace of justification; for *if it is by grace, it is no longer on the basis of works, otherwise (as the same Apostle says) grace would no longer be grace.*
>
> (IX) But though it is necessary to believe that sins are not forgiven, nor have they ever been forgiven, save freely by the divine mercy on account of Christ; nevertheless, it must not be said that anyone's sins are or have been forgiven simply because he has a proud assurance and certainty that they have been forgiven, and relies solely on that. For this empty and ungodly assurance may exist among heretics and schismatics, as indeed it

does exist in our day, and is preached most controversially against the catholic church. Neither should it be declared that those who are truly justified must determine within themselves beyond the slightest hesitation that they are justified, and that no one is absolved from sin and justified except one who believes with certainty that he has been absolved and justified, and that absolution and justification are effected by this faith alone- as if one who does not believe this is casting doubts on God's promises and on the efficacy of the death and resurrection of Christ. For, just as no devout person ought to doubt the mercy of God, the merit of Christ and the power and efficacy of the sacraments; so it is possible for anyone, while he regards himself and his own weakness and lack of dispositions, to be anxious and fearful about his own state of grace, since no one can know, by that assurance of faith which excludes all falsehood, that he has obtained the grace of God.'

Divergent denominational views on justification

So it was that, following the Council of Trent, the stage was set for the enduring polemic which continues to divide Christendom. Largely centred on the primary concern of how people are justified before God, the nature and role of faith is seen to be related in some way to scripture as well as to Christian *praxis*, to human will, and to the ecclesial ministries of magisterium and sacraments. And yet somehow these different aspects of faith resolve themselves into a single issue: given the universally acknowledged assertion that justification proceeds from faith, what part (if any) is played by human endeavour or by human cooperation with the justifying grace that faith has made accessible? Put simply, what is the relationship between faith and works? This was, and remains, a question of primary and central importance.

Few would challenge the notion that the polarization of Western Christendom into a plethora of denominations, each with its own distinctive confession of faith, was not accomplished without serious violence – not only material violence but also in terms of mutual recrimination and dearth of charity. Yet there were also positive effects as the process of 'reformation' eventually became universalized throughout Christendom and the very nature of the dialogue among the differing denominations brought about a sharper clarification of the essentials of the faith. One is left to speculate about the true impact of what today would be called 'ecumenical dialogue' in the centuries immediately following the Reformation, for as the denominational differences became ever clearer, some surprising new insights emerged about the spirituality and practice of the Christian faith.

A case in point would be those denominations which, unlike the Lutherans, followed the logic of justification by faith (alone) to a form of Augustinian predestination. John Calvin's theocratic hold over Geneva is, perhaps, the most famous exemplar of this particular fruit of the Reformation, but the speculative thought of Huldrych Zwingli and the Reformation principles he established at Zürich also provide a fascinating window onto some surprising vistas. Not least among them is the question of the relationship between faith and good works in the context of a particular and radical view of grace that sees God's providence as so pervasive in the world as to be nearly deterministic.

From a Zwinglian perspective, then, we might expect any extolling of human free will to be pointless or, worse, rooted in the ignorance of idolatry; and at a superficial level this is so. On a deeper level, however, since God's providence may be understood to be all pervasive in the world, human good works may also be comfortably ascribed to it. For Zwingli, human sanctification, with attendant good works, was a welcome aspect of God's sovereignty, and this extended from the individual to an entire society (as he tried to demonstrate in Zürich). Moreover, Zwingli famously de-coupled the sacraments from any role in salvation, for to do otherwise would be to impugn both divine sovereignty and common sense. Since goodness and truth is a fundamental aspect of divine providence, with or without any sacraments, it would be perfectly possible for 'righteous pagans' who abjure the sacraments to be, nevertheless, among the elect in Christ.

Such speculative suppositions were anathema to Luther, not least because they seemed to subvert the literal sense of scripture, and there are obvious and profound differences separating Zwingli from the Catholic position. And yet ... Could Huldrych Zwingli's speculation on divine providence, human sanctification and even election speak to some striking similarities found in the second chapter of *Lumen Gentium*, the 1964 key-note document of the Second Vatican Council? The centuries-old conversation may involve an often-stressful dialectic but, for those who persevere, the harvest may also be unexpectedly fruitful.

A contemporary perspective: *Joint Declaration on the Doctrine of Justification*

A final case in point, exemplifying the progress that has been made in the long conversation, will also serve as a conclusion for this, the first part of our study, involving the modern meaning and relevance of the assertion that we are justified by faith. Coming full circle from the birth of the idea at the beginning of the Reformation, the spiritual heirs of Luther and of the Fathers who were gathered at Trent issued a *Joint Declaration on the Doctrine of Justification* in 1997 which forms an important part of a long dialogue that will, hopefully, continue into the future. In the *Joint Declaration*, many of the issues discussed in this paper were analysed, not at all in a spirit of accusation or rancour or superficial compromise. True, a number of differing emphases were acknowledged on several issues revolving around justification by faith, not least the many questions pertaining to the role of human will and the place of works. Yet an overall consensus was reached, through a shared acknowledgement of the problems of interpretation and through a common understanding that practical expressions of righteousness are, quite properly, the fruits of faith.

It must suffice here to point out just a few of the many important points articulated by the *Joint Declaration* of 1997. Its first article states with eloquent brevity both the important centrality of the issue and also the depth of the historic problem. It notes that the doctrine of justification was a central plank of the Lutheran Reformation in the sixteenth century, of which it was held to be the 'first and chief article' and the 'ruler and judge over all other Christian doctrines'. The Reformation formulation of the doctrine was particularly asserted and defended in the *Joint Declaration*, as also was its value in challenging the contemporary theology of the Roman Catholic Church – a theology that asserted and defended a rather different doctrine of justification. From the Reformation perspective, the question of justification was the crux of all the disputes. Doctrinal condemnations were put forward, both in the Lutheran confessions and by the Roman Catholic Church's Council of Trent that are still valid today and that still have a church-dividing effect.

Of further significance in the articles forming the preamble to the *Joint Declaration* is an acknowledgement of the long process of dialogue, encompassing nearly three decades, in which Lutherans and Catholics have engaged with one another on the issue of justification. Here we find a summary of the fruits of that careful and lengthy dialogue. In the following section of the *Joint Declaration*, an impressive array of biblical citations are listed that touch upon justification. It should, however, be noted that these citations are not merely presented as 'proof texts', as the second section of the document, consisting of a single article (13), makes clear.

> 'Opposing interpretations and applications of the biblical message of justification were in the sixteenth century a principle cause of the division of the Western Church and led as well to doctrinal condemnations. A common understanding of justification is therefore fundamental and indispensable to overcoming that division. By appropriating insights of recent biblical studies and drawing on modern investigations of the history of theology and dogma, the post-Vatican II ecumenical dialogue has led to a notable convergence concerning justification, with the result that this Joint Declaration is able to formulate a consensus on basic truths concerning the doctrine of justification. In light of this consensus, the corresponding

doctrinal condemnations of the sixteenth century do not apply to today's partner.'

Section three of the *Joint Document* concisely describes the nature of Lutheran-Catholic consensus on justification:

'Fundamentally based on a joint understanding of scripture, there is consensus between Lutherans and Catholics on the meaning of justification that is not subverted by differing explications in particular statements.

'Justification is the work of the Triune God founded on the death and resurrection of Christ, thus Christ himself is our righteousness, shared through the Holy Spirit in accord with the will of the Father. Lutherans and Catholics confess together that justification is God's gift of grace and is not based on human merit *but* it equips and calls us to good works.

'All are called to God for salvation in Christ whom we receive through faith, which is itself a gift, given by the Holy Spirit working through word and sacrament in the community of believers and, at the same time, leads believers to renewal of life brought to completion in eternal life.

'The message of justification goes to the heart of the New Testament message of God's saving mercy through Christ. That new life is solely due to the mercy of God, imparted as a gift and not merited in any way.

'Therefore, the doctrine of justification, which takes up this message and explicates it, is more than just one part of Christian doctrine. It stands in an essential relation to all truths of faith, which are to be seen as internally related to each other. It is an indispensable criterion which constantly serves to orient all the teaching and practice of our churches to Christ. When Lutherans emphasize the unique significance of this criterion, they do not deny the interrelation and significance of all truths of faith. When Catholics see themselves as bound by several criteria, they do not deny the special function of the message of justification. Lutherans and Catholics share the goal of confessing Christ, who is to be trusted above all things as the one Mediator ... through whom God in the Holy Spirit gives himself and pours out his renewing gifts.'

The final section of the *Joint Document* (articles 19-44) offers an explication of the consensus noted above and provides both Lutheran and Catholic emphases and nuances on commonly held positions regarding justification. It is, perhaps, the continuing sense of passion by which human justification before God is understood, leading from the thought-provoking doctrinal polemic of the Reformation to a modern application of profound dialogue, that has made possible what would once have been unthinkable: the imminent visit of the head of the Roman Catholic Church, Pope Francis, to celebrate the five hundredth anniversary of the Reformation with the Lutheran inhabitants of Lund, Sweden on 31 October 2017.

Faith and works in the New Covenant

The final part of this analysis will seek briefly to address an aspect of the assertion that we are justified by faith which is as relevant to modern concerns as ever it was in the past: how can one simultaneously claim that justification is *vicarious*, in the sense of being the freely given gift of God without recourse to any merit of our own, and at the same time assert the necessity of human freedom and cooperation in that process? That this is an urgent modern concern can be demonstrated by its antithesis, for a host of dehumanizing tendencies has left many people feeling alienated, disenfranchised and disempowered on both a social and psychological level. A concrete expression of Christian *praxis*, animated by a faith that is neither conceived of nor experienced abstractly, has often acted as an antidote to this malaise and continues to do so. Furthermore, there is an increasingly prevalent tendency to view a perceived dichotomy between 'faith', often expressed in terms of words, and 'action', expressed as deeds, as mere hypocrisy. Terrorists wagging moralizing fingers and yammering about God's will on the evening news are often discovered, when apprehended, with computers loaded with pornography. A well-known American evangelical preacher blamed the events of 9/11 on national sinfulness (and, by extrapolation, on God) as the whole world listened in gap-mouthed wonder. And, of course, various scandals and forms of in-fighting seem to emanate from the Vatican today, even as they did five hundred years ago. The modern world is looking for clear evidence that the Gospel of Jesus Christ does, indeed, have the power to save.

Perhaps an answer to the conundrum that acknowledges and honours *both* the necessary sovereignty of God *and* the imperative of human *praxis* in the process of salvation can be found in that rich fabric of Christian tradition that is less the purview of dogmatic theology than of spirituality. I refer to mysticism. Beginning, as did Martin Luther, with Paul's letter to the Romans, it is abundantly evident that, in Paul's understanding, humanity could not be saved simply by observance of the Law - not because such an observance would be inherently incapable of salvation but because it was not possible for humanity, burdened by an impaired will, to do so. From the sixteenth century to the present, all the various denominations in the Western Church have concurred with this basic biblical supposition. But Paul goes on to say in Romans that the Law is not nullified but is *established*; and this is preceded by the admonition (significantly quoted from the Old Testament) that '[God] will render to every man according to his deeds'.

For Paul, then, the concrete *praxis* of discipleship possesses a mystical quality which, in turn, is expressed as a kind of existential immediacy in which the 'fused' lives of the risen Christ and the individual believer can deliver the same soteriological consequences as a strict obedience to the Law. This is surely the only possible explanation for Paul's otherwise outrageous statement that '… in my flesh I do my share in … filling up what is lacking in Christ's afflictions'. This mystical life is characterized by the triple qualities of 'suffering', 'consolation' and 'exhortation', and it represents the goal and summit of Christian discipleship. That this speaks to a kind of 'works-orientated' soteriology seems clear; but, to paraphrase Paul, there is no room for boasting because the merit is not ours to possess. Rather, it is that of Christ's death and risen life, mediated to the believer by faith.

A similar insight is found in the life and experience of Augustine of Hippo, who is hugely influential among both Catholics and many of the principal sixteenth century reformers alike. It should be said at the outset that no-one can accuse Augustine of espousing a works-driven route to salvation that is reliant in any way upon human merit. His regard for the utter sovereignty of God, not least in respect to human salvation, led him to espouse a doctrine of elective predestination substantially similar to that of Zwingli and Calvin nearly twelve hundred years later.

Moreover, Augustine dwelt at great length in his classic spiritual autobiography, *Confessions*, upon the tendency toward sinfulness (disordered desire) that had paralysed his free-will even to the extent that his life was driven by trivial and destructive pursuits that kept him in a permanent state of fearful anxiety. It was only through the subjective experience of interior illumination, clearly understood as the gift of an invitation by Christ to enter into a living faith with him, that Augustine could, paradoxically, claim the absolute freedom of action. It corresponded to Paul's insight, echoed generations before Augustine, that true freedom of action – that is, the freedom to act in ways that one knows to be pure - is only made possible by a will made obedient by divine grace. Augustine is then able to famously write, 'Love and do what you want', for it is through faith and the agency of God's grace that the human will is orientated in a way that had been impossible before.

Augustine now discovers to his delight - as Paul did before him - that God has issued an invitation to a kind of partnership. Humans can now follow the path of love. It is what they were made for. When sin obscures the source and essence of that love, what follows is a 'false love' (concupiscence). By contrast, divine grace, made accessible by faith, reveals 'true love' (God); and through this reorientation the will is enabled to do what it always wanted to do but had, in its unilluminated state, found impossible.

Faith and works in the High Medieval period

Finally, we should take into account the rich contemplative legacy of the High Medieval period, particularly the fresh insights and emphases of the twelfth century. Here, the affective quality of Christian *praxis*, already eloquently attested to by Paul and Augustine in both its inward and outward manifestations, comes to its greatest flowering; and in doing so, it sheds it brightest rays of light on the question of a harmonious relationship between faith and works – or, to put it in a slightly different way, between divine sovereignty and human agency.

Bernard of Clairvaux, identified by Dante (through Beatrice) as a 'spiritual guide', never ceases to stress the affective quality of God's call and the human response to it. His *Homilies on the Song of Songs* identify and re-interpret that ancient aspect of unitive soteriology - witnessed to by Christ, Paul, Augustine and many other spiritual giants in the Christian tradition - based on the powerful metaphor of conjugal love. It can only be conceived of in terms of partnership. Bernard also respects and acknowledges the sovereignty of God, which leads him to a conclusion shared alike by Catholics and the reformers of the sixteenth century. In his treatise *On Conversion*, published in Paris in 1140, Bernard maps the stages of human conversion, and it is significant that he begins with an undeserved, perhaps even unexpected, act of the divine will that calls the perceptive Christian 'with an inner voice'.

Within the early Cistercian period, mention should also be made of Aelred of Rievaulx. With a kind of gentle earthiness, Aelred fearlessly traverses a theological minefield by likening human relationships to the love of God. Though there had been antecedents, notably in Augustine and Paulinus of Nola, there was also a strong reluctance to conflate human and divine love. To do so seemed fraught with difficulties. Augustine, this time in a treatise on the death of a friend, cites examples given by the Desert Fathers. Aiming at purity of heart yet conscious of the monastic fear of homosexuality, they were, in different ways, wary of too close an identification of divine and human love. Aelred, nevertheless, forges a spirituality in which God is seen as friendship. In his introduction to Aelred's classic work, *Spiritual Friendship*, Douglass Roby writes:

> 'Aelred looked at friendship from the divine perspective, insisting that it springs directly from God, who in the overflowing of his love created men to share his love by loving each other and himself. This opportunity for love, which extends to a certain extent even to irrational creatures, is the particular glory of men and angels. Man's nature thus requires that he be a loving as well as rational creature.'

Perhaps the greatest of the spiritual masters of the twelfth century who may shed light on the properly understood relationship of faith and works is the 12th century Scottish Augustinian, Richard of St. Victor. In his work *Concerning the Trinity*, Richard offers a 'proof' of God's triune existence based on the scriptural assertion that 'God is love'. That aspect of divine love - not understood as a mere ethic, but as the very nature of the Godhead - expresses itself, first, in a community of Persons (Father, Son, and Holy Spirit) comprising the Godhead. Then, because it is infinite in nature, divine love expresses itself also in the over-flowing act of creation, so that creature and Creator have a real and direct affinity with one another in terms of the essence of God's being. Richard of St Victor describes God as being the 'self-diffusive Good', and his conception is wholly dynamic as the lover and the beloved constantly seek one another out. Building on this foundation, and fully conscious of the illumination experienced by Augustine before him, Richard then describes the contemplative life in those terms. The soul is predisposed to God's illuminating grace, described in affective terms, and the direction and reciprocation of that illuminative grace is also described in affective terms.

A conclusion

Foundational for Paul, Augustine and the twelfth-century contemplatives, the Gospel injunction to love God and one another is observed. This is the fulfilment of the Law of the Old Covenant and the single commandment of the New Covenant. The ability to observe that

Law was realized by Christ, perfected on the Cross and given to believers as the grace of conversion through faith in Christ. However one understands the re-animation of the human will as a product of redemption from sin, it seems that it would be folly to negate the efficacy of works *provided* we understand that such works are not merely our own but the works of Christ himself. They are the indwelling of the one animated by God's freely given and sanctifying grace. Thus, as the faith that justifies is understood to be a gift freely given by God and owing nothing to human merit, so good works can be understood in the same way; as the fruit of that initial gift given by God, performed in and through us by the indwelling Christ, as mediated by the grace imparted by the Holy Spirit.

4

Creeds: is it still possible to say them without denying one's intellect?
by Professor Frances Young
Emeritus Professor of Theology, Birmingham University

Talk given at St Peter's Methodist Church, Canterbury, 25 October 2017

This is, of course, a long-standing question. Many years ago, in a little book called, *Can these dry bones live?* (SCM press, 1982), I quoted a letter that I had received from a lifelong lay Christian, an ordinary man who left school at 14, had no educational advantages, and had worked hard all his life at very ordinary jobs. He really cared about integrity and honesty. Here is something of what he wrote:

> 'It is unfortunate but nevertheless a fact that the Christian church as a whole is losing ground so far as active membership is concerned, simply because on conscience grounds they cannot any longer keep up a charade. I know from personal experience how difficult it is to support certain dogmas today.'

He acknowledged that there had been much progress since science became the 'central pivot of human understanding', and he had met many thoughtful people over the years who wanted the truth. He thought fundamentalism was being challenged as never before, and felt this was to be welcomed, for it indicated that a renewed search for truth was replacing dogmatic demands that had caused so much frustration.

So let's start by clarifying the issues.

What exactly is the problem with the creeds?

The first problem is probably the scientific understanding to which my old correspondent referred. The obvious issues are questions about creation (in the light of Darwinism), about the virgin birth (in the light of modern genetics), and about the resurrection of the flesh (in the light of modern biochemistry).

The second problem is the emphasis on factuality and literalism in our culture and language – often at a very crude level. After all, a huge amount of language is metaphorical or symbolic. My kids used to love expressions like, 'Mum's climbing up the wall'. The intellect has been narrowed down to one kind of rationality, straight logic and concrete facts. This is ironical in the age of film, fiction and fantasy, especially with the advent of computer games, virtual reality, and so on. In any case, science itself uses metaphors and models, stretching language from its ordinary sense so as to express deeper and wider concepts. People may think there is a split between the head and the heart, but in fact 'knowing' and 'understanding' - both emotionally and intellectually - involve complex brain functions with both the left and right brain working together. Truth is bigger than fact, and language is more subtle than literal. Let me share a few reflections from a little novel by Graham Swift, *Mothering Sunday*, published earlier this year. It's about a young woman, Jane Fairchild, who is a maid in a middle-class English household in the 1920s who finds herself involved sexually with the soon-to-be-married son of a neighbouring family. Later in her life she becomes a noted writer. Through Jane, Swift reflects upon the nature of stories.

> 'There was something more enticing about calling something a tale rather than a story, but this had to do, perhaps, with the suggestion that it might not be wholly truthful, it might have a larger element of invention. About all these words – tale, story, even narrative – there was a sort of question, always hovering in the background, of truth, and it might be hard to say how much truth went with each. There was also the word "fiction"… which could seem almost totally dismissive of truth. A complete fiction! Yet something that was clearly and completely fiction could also contain – this was the nub and the mystery of the matter – truth….

'Telling stories, telling tales. Always the implication that you were trading in lies. But for her [Jane Fairchild] it would always be the task of getting to the quick, the heart, the nub, the pith: the trade of truth telling … So what was it exactly then, this truth telling? … It was about being true to the very stuff of life, it was about trying to capture, though you never could, the very feel of being alive. It was about finding a language. And it was about being true to the fact, the one thing only followed from the other, that many things in life – oh so many more than we think – can never be explained at all.'

And a third problem with the creeds is the contemporary issue of individualism: that is to say, the emphasis on self-responsible independence, the way we make our own truth, our own reality, our own morality – the modern sense of autonomy, of not being subject to any authority. This first-person standpoint, in which *my* way of seeing things is of paramount importance, is what gives rise to the problem of intellectual integrity: can *I* sign up to it, whatever anyone else may believe? As the quotes from my old correspondent indicate, loads of people haven't been able to sign up to the Christian faith expressed in the creeds because it's not *my* truth. No one likes dogma. No one likes to be told what they should think.

And that leads us into the second issue.

The problem of dogma/doctrine

People are uncomfortable with dogmatic truth enforced by authority, and they assume that this is what the creeds are supposed to be. The Thirty-Nine Articles of Religion, promulgated at the time of the Reformation, were propositions to which you had to be committed, definitions of belief. So are the creeds the same?

Well, the Greek word *dogma* and the Latin word *doctrina* simply mean 'teaching'. In ancient philosophy, at the time of the rise of Christianity, the main element of each teaching was a way of life – ethics - plus an account of how the world provides the context and justification for the way of life taught. Stoicism, for example, said that you should 'live according to nature'. For the Stoics, nature meant a great cosmic spirit or fire, and it was living in tune with this that lay at the heart of their wisdom and advice. Epicureanism enjoined the pleasure principle, suggesting that since everything is just made of atoms, arbitrarily colliding and combining, how you chose to spend your life was a matter of cosmic indifference.

In line with this approach, early Christianity can be described in broad terms as teaching that: 'Christians live like this because God is the creator of everything, God sees into your very heart, and God judges the secrets therein.' Or: 'Christians live like this because they are set free by Christ from everything that has gone wrong with humanity.' Or: 'Christians live like this because in baptism they have been cleansed and given new life by the Spirit.' Or: 'Christians live like this because Christ has overcome death, and so you should keep your bodies pure for the life of the world to come.'

These kinds of statements about how Christians should live were reinforced by the overarching story of Scripture, from the beginning to the end, into which a convert's life should fit – each one being taken up into something bigger than themselves. *Dogma*, meaning 'teaching', was not a series of definitions or propositions or formulae, but stories or 'myths' about the way things are. Stories in this sense are not 'trading in lies' but are 'getting to the quick, the heart, the nub, the pith: the trade of truth-telling'; and myths are not invented accounts of things that never really happened, but religious stories explaining life, the universe and everything.

Let me offer a short digression on definitions. Is it possible to define God? To 'de-fine' means, literally, to limit. Thus, to try to de-fine God is to try to limit the divine. In the 4th century the notion of the Trinity was articulated and defended *against* people who wanted to define God. The Syrian Christian poet, Ephrem, is well worth quoting.

Whoever is capable of investigating becomes the container of what he investigates; a knowledge which is capable of containing the Omniscient is greater than Him, for it has proved capable of measuring the whole of Him.

A person who investigates the Father and Son is thus greater than them!

Far be it, then, and something anathema, that the Father and Son should be investigated, while dust and ashes exults itself!

In other words, it is all too easy to reduce God to the size of our own minds. So Ephrem spells out the way in which metaphors and symbols and parables – the language of Scripture – creates a garment of names.

Let us give thanks to God who clothed Himself in the names of the body's various parts:

Scripture refers to His 'ears', to teach us that he listens to us; it speaks of His 'eyes', to show that He sees us.

It was just the names of such things that He put on, and, although in His true Being there is not wrath or regret, yet He put on these names too because of our weakness.

Refrain: Blessed is He who has appeared to our human race under so many metaphors.

After several stanzas developing such points, Ephrem tells a parable about someone trying to teach a parrot to talk, and holding a mirror in front of his face so that the parrot looks into the mirror and thinks it is conversing with one of its own kind. That is the kind of thing God had to do to communicate with us, he suggests. You cannot define God. Ephrem admits:

There is intellectual enquiry in the Church, investigating what is revealed: the intellect was not intended to pry into hidden things.

Creeds – what sort of things are they?

Well, creeds were never definitions or articles of belief, though they did become tests of orthodoxy.

The first thing to notice is their liturgical context. In the fourth century we have evidence of many local creeds in use, but universally they had a three-part shape, which seems to derive from the confessions used at baptism. They were learnt by heart during catechesis to be recited in the baptismal liturgy. In the 4th century, bishops meeting in Council sought to prove their orthodoxy by reciting whichever creed they had learnt and recited at their baptism. At the Council of Nicaea in 325, one such creed was adopted as the basis of an agreed statement into which certain terms were inserted to ensure an orthodox understanding. In 381 at the Council of Constantinople, the decisions of Nicaea were re-affirmed, but the creed that was adopted there, now known as the Nicene Creed, was actually a different local creed with Nicene insertions and other extra material at certain key points.

The three-part form derives from an earlier pattern in which three questions were asked as the actual baptism happened.

> Do you believe in God, the Father Almighty?

> Do you believe in Christ Jesus, the Son of God, who was born of the Holy Ghost of the Virgin Mary, and was crucified under Pontius Pilate, and was dead and buried, and rose again the third day, alive from the dead, and ascended into heaven, and sat at the right hand of the Father, and will come to judge the quick and the dead?

> Do you believe in the Holy Ghost, and the holy church, and the resurrection of the flesh?

After each response, and therefore three times in all, the candidate was dipped into the water and submerged. The custom was no doubt based on the dominical command to baptise in the name of the Father, the Son and the Holy Spirit (Matthew 28:19).

If we go back earlier still we find many catchphrases in the New Testament, which are taken up in the creed-like summaries that are found in some second century documents. This example is from Ignatius's *Letter to the Trallians*, Chapter 9:

> 'Be deaf when everyone speaks to you apart from Jesus Christ, who was of the stock of David, who was from Mary, who was truly born, ate and drank, was truly persecuted under Pontius Pilate, was truly crucified and died in the sight of beings heavenly, earthly and under the earth, who also was truly raised from the dead, His Father raising him ...'

Clearly, passages such as this constituted the traditional 'in-language' of the early Christian communities. Compare, for example, Ignatius's words with those of Paul in his *Letter to the Romans*, 1:3ff:

> '... concerning his Son, who was born of David's seed according to the flesh, who was declared Son of God with power by the Spirit of Holiness when he was raised from the dead, Jesus Christ our Lord, through whom we have received grace ...'

What we see here is a stereotyped confessional language affirming loyalty to Christ and to the God who sent him. These statements are parallel to the sort of confessions we find in the Old Testament, for example in Deuteronomy 5:4 and Deuteronomy 26:5ff. By the second century we find various summary statements of the Christian faith that follow roughly the same threefold pattern: they are called either the Rule of Faith or the Canon of Truth. They are not word-for-word the same, but freely composed summaries in various writings, containing much of the 'in-language' which would feature in the later creeds. So here are two roots of the creeds which have come down to us: confessional summaries and baptismal liturgies.

By the early 4th century the practice was established of catechesis through Lent followed by baptism on Easter eve, so that the candidate rose with Christ on Easter morning. During catechesis there was a 'handing over' of the creed (learning it by heart and hearing commentary on it), and then its 'giving back' in the baptismal liturgy when the candidate recited it. In catechetical lectures surviving from this period, the creeds are called a summary of the Scriptures, given to converts since not everyone could read them for themselves. This implies that they provided the key moments in the overarching story of the Bible. But notice what's missing: the long historical narratives of Israel, most of the prophetic material except as fulfilled in Christ, and the actual life and teaching of Jesus. Rather, the focus is entirely on his birth, death and resurrection. The message is clear: what is key for the Christian faith is the beginning (creation), the middle (Christ), and the end (the consummation of all things).

So what is the genre of the creeds? They are more like an ancient hymn than anything else, something like the *Te Deum* or the *Gloria*, a liturgical remembering and reminding. There is no actual dogma or doctrine of the Trinity, no Christology in the theoretical sense, no atonement theory. We do not have here propositions or articles of belief, but confessions of faith and trust and loyalty – a celebration in community of the way the world is, which then provides the context for a lifestyle distinct from that of the world.

Why is it important to keep saying the creeds?

The first reason, I suggest, is that in saying them we affirm the importance of belonging to the community, of our identity as Christians. It's about ecumenism, not just between different Christian traditions in different places in our own time, but different Christians over time, over the centuries, recognising that we are part of something bigger than ourselves. It's about commitment; it takes us beyond our self-sufficiency, beyond the narrowness of 'my' truth. Indeed, it implies nothing less than an entire overarching story in which the whole thing hangs together and the constituent bits of it are not there to be picked off. You can't say, 'This is okay but not that', worrying about the virgin birth, say, or the resurrection of the flesh. The creed offers an all-embracing story that makes sense of life, the universe and everything – even of oneself.

The creed, then, is a classic case of allowing language to be *stretched* to speak of larger truths than the immediate, simple or obvious meaning. God is a God *beyond*, and yet God's very self is present in the human life of Jesus and all that was entailed in it. The creed cannot necessarily be expressed or understood in limited human language.

So, what about those sticking-points?

I suppose the obvious ones are creation, the virgin birth, and the resurrection of the flesh. So I offer a few comments on these, particularly the importance of their hanging together.

Creation, I believe, was the very first 'doctrine' to be established, and it was important in making Christianity distinctive in the context of the ancient world. The argument went like this. God cannot have made everything out of some stuff or matter which pre-existed, or God would not be the sole first principle. God cannot have made everything out of God's self or everything would be God. It follows, then, that God must have made everything *out of nothing*. The importance of this was that the material, the physical, the fleshly, could never be dismissed as evil; it was fundamentally good, because it was entirely God's creation. So there could be no separation of the soul or spirit from the physical and the bodily, as many were propounding in the second century.

The consequence of this affirmation of the physical and material is that sacramentalism lies at the very heart of early Christianity: Helena, the wife of Constantine (the first Christian Emperor), took a cartload of earth from the Holy Land back to her palace in Rome, so that she could pray on ground on which the feet of the incarnate Christ had trodden. Water, bread and wine, oil – these become the vehicle of the holy in the context of liturgy. And it was this emphasis on material physicality that explains why the notion of the resurrection of the flesh, the body, held a greater significance for Christianity than the immortality of the soul. Already in the second century it was being argued that a human being is created as a unity comprising both soul and body; and it is the *whole* created human person, not a bit of it, that is raised to new life. Indeed, in I Corinthians 15 Paul had already anticipated that point, with his idea of resurrection requiring a spiritual body.

So finally, what about the virgin birth and our knowledge of genetics – the fact that Jesus could not have been a normal human being without DNA from a human father? May I suggest that the story was never meant to be taken in terms of biology? Indeed, there was deep resistance in the early church to treating it as if it was a myth like those of the gods of the Greeks, where, for example, Zeus would have had physical intercourse with a human to produce some great hero like Heracles.

Several observations may help here.

Firstly, in Jewish tradition the creation of a new human being involved the man and the woman, and 'the Holy One, blessed be he.' The crucial thing was Mary's obedience at the annunciation.

Secondly, the Hebrew word in Isaiah's prophecy, translated as 'virgin' in Greek and English, meant no more than a 'young maiden'. The Jewish scholar, Geza Vermes, suggested that, whereas most miraculous births in the Old Testament happened to old women, sometimes beyond child-bearing age and often previously barren throughout life, the miracle of Jesus's birth was understood as a miracle of newness, birth to a pre-menstrual girl, too young to bear a child.

And thirdly, in Luke's Gospel the Holy Spirit 'hovers over' or 'overshadows' Mary, just as the Holy Spirit overshadowed the chaos in the Genesis creation-story. This story is about new creation in Christ – humanity renewed. So without attempting to spell out a theory or a dogma, we can begin to see how the story of the virgin birth coheres with those other key features of Christianity – that insistence on the physical reality of the incarnation, and of the genuineness of the passion, all of which fits with the goodness of the material creation, the story of its redemption and resurrection, and its sacramental efficacy in the context of liturgy.

5

Jesus: How can we understand that he is the saviour of the world?
by Rt. Revd. Michael Nazir-Ali
President of OXTRAD and former Bishop of Rochester

Talk given at St Peter's Methodist Church, Canterbury, 27 September 2017

Dr George Carey once told the story of an encounter that he had on a train with someone who, noticing his dog collar, said how much he admired Jesus the man and his teaching. After some conversation, George said to him: 'Well of course it's not just that he is a man, but we also believe that he is God with us'. The man drew back immediately and said: 'There we must differ', and rather stiffly got off the train. I hope the train had stopped by then! That does remind us, I think, of how people, certainly in the Western world, think of Jesus. There is a kind of vestigial and affectionate memory of him. This came home to me some time ago when I sponsored a debate in the House of Lords on the role of religion in society, and the civil servants dealing with the debate said: 'Well, Bishop, the person who will be speaking immediately after you is a leading atheist and he will try and negate what you are going to say'. The peer certainly rubbished much of what I had said, but then, at the very end of his speech, he played into my hands by saying: 'When I have to decide what to do, I always think of the Sermon on the Mount'.

He was not alone: time and again we find people who admire Jesus the man and who think they know something of his teaching; but as with this peer who, when he talked of the Sermon on the Mount actually meant the beatitudes, many people have no more than a vestigial sense of the true significance of Jesus. Philip Pullman's book on Jesus is another example of how people admire Jesus but are wary of any doctrinal claims about him.

Other faiths and Jesus

And then there are the views of other religions about Jesus. Islam certainly knows about Jesus, and if you ask me what Muslim tradition believes about him, I would say there are three things. Firstly, according to the Qur'an, Jesus was the word and spirit of God. He was a prophet and apostle who works miracles, dies and rises again (in some unspecified way) and ascends to heaven. Secondly, in the *Ahadīth*, a collection of traditions claiming to report the words and actions of the prophet Muhammed, the emphasis is more on the things that Jesus will do when he comes back. In particular, he will convert all of Christendom to Islam and he will pray behind the prophet Muhammed. And thirdly, there is the mystical aspect of Sufism that sees Jesus as an icon of asceticism – of giving up everything for God and of being prepared to suffer for God's sake.

In a different faith context, Hinduism regards Jesus as *Sadguru* – a true guru who is the incarnation of one or other god and who leads people into the pathways of truth. He is not, in this respect, unique in Hindu culture, but it is certainly quite possible for Hindus to follow Jesus as a guide into the ways of truth. Indeed, for some, he may become the sole focus of worship.

And then there is, of course, the Jewish view of Jesus, which has changed over the centuries as Christian-Jewish relationships have changed. So in *Toledoth Yeshu*, an early Jewish text about the life of Jesus, we find that he is portrayed as an illegitimate child who practised magic and heresy and died a shameful death; and the *Talmud*, a central text of rabbinic Judaism, tells us that Jesus was killed because he had deceived the people. But then, more recently, we find a reassessment or review of what Jews think about Jesus and an attempt to claim him back, as it were, if not for Judaism at least for Jewishness. So the Jewishness of Jesus is now an important aspect of the study of his person; but these reassessments don't agree with one another. There is, for example, Geza Vermes's attempt to show Jesus as *Hāsīd*, a pious Jew wholly of his time who taught and worked miracles in the way that *Hasīdīm* typically did.

On the other hand there is the Reformed Jewish rabbi Dan Cohn Sherbok's assessment, which regards Jesus as a prophet of the Old Testament type. And then there is Pinchas Lapide, a Jewish theologian and Israeli historian, who is willing to believe in the resurrection of Jesus as God's vindication of faithfulness.

The divinity of Jesus

So different traditions and religions hold different views about Jesus; but for Christians the key question is: What did Jesus say about himself? He talked about the fulfilment of the times, about the nearness of the kingdom of God, and about the need for people to repent of their sins; but did he himself feature in the good news that he was proclaiming? Here, too, there are disagreements. James Dunn, a New Testament scholar and now emeritus professor at Durham, concluded that Jesus was not in any way the content of his own preaching.

For myself, I, like many others, prefer to take the line that C H Dodd took in many of his books in the mid-20th century, namely that Jesus not only preached the kingdom of God but also saw himself as embodying that kingdom. For example, he called people to follow him and to take his yoke upon themselves because he was meek and humble of heart. Jesus's consciousness of his intimacy with his Father, his awareness of his fulfilment of prophecy, and his tendency to forgive sins are further ways in which he figures in his own preaching.

But I come back to the question: what did Jesus actually think of himself? Did he actually see himself as divine? These are huge questions that could keep us here all night, but I will give a few examples. Some years ago there was a television series by Rageh Omar on *The Miracles of Jesus*. There are two billion Christians in the world, but the BBC (in their impartial way) chose a Muslim as the presenter of a series that turned out to be very interesting indeed. To be honest, Omar was actually more credible than some radical Christian scholars might have been. He thought, for example, that Jesus was revealing his own understanding of himself through his miracles. The nature miracles, such as the stilling of the storm, were declaring his divinity because he had control of nature. In the healing miracles, likewise, Jesus told people like the paralytic man that their sins were forgiven, and he did this in a number of instances.

Then there are the exorcisms, where Jesus showed his command of the supernatural as well as the natural world. Rageh Omar thought that such miracles were vehicles of Jesus's claim to divinity; and he went on to say that it was precisely for this reason that the Qur'an did not emphasize them. Personally, I think that he was wrong about this, because in fact the Qur'an talks about the miracles of Jesus in some detail. Some of the miracles recorded in the Qur'an are also mentioned in the canonical Gospels while others come from apocryphal material, particularly the Arabic Infancy Gospel.

There are other examples. Vinoth Ramachandra, a Sri Lankan theologian, pointed out in his London Institute for Contemporary Christianity lectures that Jesus also thought of himself as the divine Wisdom. The examples he gave are in Matthew 11 where the disciples of John come to Jesus and say: 'Are you the one we are looking for or should we look for someone else?' By way of reply, Jesus refers them to what is happening in his ministry: the deaf are hearing, the lame are walking, the blind are seeing, the lepers are cured. He says: 'Blessed are those who take no offence at me' – a reference that harks back to the passage in Isaiah 35 which is about the coming of *God*. And then, when he is talking to the crowds about John the Baptist, Jesus goes on to talk about his own ministry and how people are turning away from him. 'But wisdom is justified by her deeds' he says, referring to himself and his work. Again, in the next chapter of Matthew (chapter 12), Jesus says that 'the Queen of the South came to hear the Wisdom of Solomon' but that 'here is someone greater than Solomon'. What or who is greater than Solomon in his wisdom? Well of course it is the Wisdom of God, that Wisdom from the beginning with God through whom the world was made; and it is here that Wisdom Christology and Logos Christology come very close together.

Jesus and 'the Son of Man'?

But I must move on. What are we to make of the phrase: 'The Son of Man'? When Jesus used this term, to whom was he referring? Was he referring to human beings in general, or to himself in particular, or to some other apocalyptic figure? Specifically, was Jesus referring to himself in the sense of the heavenly being who appears in Daniel 7? Professor Charlie Moule, back I think in 1974, pointed out that the interesting thing about the title 'The Son of Man' is the definite article. '*The* Son of Man', not '*Any* Son of Man': *ho huios tou anthrōpou*.

In his 2006 book *Chaos and the Son of Man*, Andy Angel, a New Testament scholar at St John's College, Nottingham, examined the way in which Aramaic developed in the first three centuries of our era, and he pointed out that if the evangelists had wanted to record Jesus as saying something that was simply generic, as referring to humans in general or to himself as an instance of humanity, it would have been quite possible for them to translate his Aramaic words into Greek without the definite article: *huios anthrōpou*. The fact that they did not do this suggested to Angel that Jesus was using the emphatic form of Aramaic to denote a *particular* 'Son of Man' - no doubt 'The Son of Man' in Daniel 7. One of the things that I say about the Aramaic of Daniel 7, by the way, is that there is a telling verb in the sentence: 'All nations shall come and serve him or worship him'. The Aramaic word *Yaflehūn* means 'the service of God', and this is said about the Divine Son of Man; so I think it is quite important for us to relate Daniel 7 to Jesus's understanding of himself.

Jesus and the Messiahship

What about the word Messiah? Well, we all know of Jesus's reluctance to let people apply the title to him, and we know his reasons for this. The expectation at the time was that the Messiah would be a figure who, perhaps by military might and certainly by political power, would overcome Israel's enemies and restore the kingdom to Israel. Jesus wanted to distance himself from such ideas of Messiahship. He had his own vision of how, through suffering, he would establish God's kingdom, and God would vindicate him in this.

I think that is true. Professor Tom Wright, in his 1996 book *Jesus and the Victory of God,* points out that in Jesus's time the idea of the Messiah was that of a human figure. While this may well be the case in New Testament times, it was not wholly the case where the Old Testament is concerned. For example, in Ezekiel or in Psalm 89 or indeed in Psalm 2 the Messiah is more than human: he is the Divine King. Tom Wright also points to Psalm 45, which is referred to in the New Testament and which says of the Messiah: 'Your Throne, O God, is for ever and ever'. So it may be the case that Jesus's reluctance to endorse the contemporary view of Messiahship had not only to do with the military or political implications of the title but also that it reflected the inadequacy of the description of who he was. It did not encompass a full understanding of his person. Indeed, contemporary, or near contemporary apocalyptic also has a coalescing of the Son of Man and the Messiah figures into a seemingly divine being.

The sacrificial work of Jesus in a fractured world

We must also note, however, that we cannot come to understand the person of Jesus without also looking at his work, and to do that we have to reflect upon the fractured world in which we live. Many thinkers over the last two hundred years have shown us how our world and we ourselves are broken. Hegel, for instance, so influential even today, pointed out that human beings are characterized by their conflict with the world, conflict with nature, and even conflict with the very source and ground of our being. His solution to the problem of conflict in the human mind (and indeed in the universe) lay in the dialectical process of thesis, antithesis and synthesis.

Then we have the alienation that Marx spoke of – an alienation characterized by the distance between the workers and the things they made, which belonged not to them but to the capitalist who employed them.Workers, Marx noted, are also alienated from each other, for it is in keeping them unorganised that efficiency increases and the wealth of the owners expands. And then we have Freud and his theory of psychoanalysis which points us to the inner cleavage that is in us all and how that has to be overcome.

The noted 20th century theologian Frederick Dillistone pointed out some years ago that this sense of disruption in our lives and in the universe is not just a modern idea. It was something the ancients knew about, and from it arose what some have called a collective 'nostalgia for paradise' – the idea, that is, that somehow the disruption must be undone so that we can return to an original state of idyllic harmony. Dillistone observed that the great sacrificial systems of the world originated and developed in the hope of achieving this. He gave three widespread examples from Egypt, India and China of the offering of sacrifices of cereals, libations, or even animals as a means of restoring the original harmony that had been lost.

In the Bible, by contrast, things are different: here, we do not find sacrifices for the sake of, for example, restoring fertility. The Bible speaks of two kinds of sacrifice: those that celebrate God's deliverance and liberation of his people, often through a common ritual meal such as the Passover, and those that are offered for the expiation of sin. The Bible uses different names for these sacrifices, and it is important to remember that at least two of the names for sin offerings are exactly the same as those for the sins for which they are being offered.

Yet there is a tension in the Bible between seeing sacrifices as a way of establishing communion with God and the realization that such sacrifices are not enough. Over time, we find a gradually emerging view among the Old Testament prophets that the real sacrifices required by God have to do with self offering: 'a broken spirit and a contrite heart, O God, you will not despise' (Psalm 51:17). The idea of the offering up of *oneself* in obedience to God comes to a head in the great Psalm 40 where the speaker says: 'sacrifices and offerings you have not desired but you have given me a body. I have come to do your will O Lord'. Later, the writer of the letter to the Hebrews picks this up and applies it to the work of Jesus Christ.

So what we have in the work of Christ is a coming together of all the longings in the mythologies and the expectations of humankind. They all cohere in an historical event and a human person. Now, it is true to say that the suffering and death of Jesus can be experienced inwardly by believers in at least two ways: firstly in the sense that they are examples that we ourselves are to imitate ('take up your cross and follow me'), and secondly in the sense that the cross reveals to us the full extent of God's love. For Christians, these are two valuable ways of understanding the suffering of Jesus; but by themselves they are not enough. We need something more than these *subjective* experiences. We need also to understand the *objective* meaning of the atonement.

The objectivity of the atonement

The church has traditionally proclaimed three important aspects of the objectivity of the atonement. The first is that in his suffering and death, Jesus is our *representative*. Of course, the same might also be said about the incarnation, because here too we see our humanity – a humanity that has been spoilt by sin and destroyed by our own rebellion - made once again in the image of the creator. That is why Jesus is called the *Eikōn*, or the image of God. This humanity comes to a climax in his obedient offering of himself as our representative, and it is that representativeness which allows *us* to partake of the benefits of what *he* has done.

But Jesus is not only a representative, he is also, secondly, a *substitute* in the sense that he does what we are inherently unable to do for ourselves because of our personal enslavement to sin. Jesus deflects God's wrath away from our wrong doing so that a new beginning is possible and we can be friends again with God. There is nothing immoral in such a picture of substitutionary atonement. Athanasius, in his book on the incarnation, tells us that Jesus died for all, and because death could not hold him, his victory is also a victory for all. It was this insight that was famously recovered by Martin Luther who based his understanding of the cross as victory on such a view. 'The harrowing of hell', celebrated in art and literature, is another picture of this victory that Jesus wins over the forces of evil.

Of course, in the patristic period and medieval times all sorts of absurdities were associated with this view of the atonement. Jesus was thought of as the 'worm on the hook' which caught the devil, or that God had handed Jesus over to the devil in return for all the people in hell. The devil thought that he'd got a good bargain until he realized that he could not hold Jesus in hell. We don't have to accept these pictures to believe in the victory of Jesus on the cross.

And thirdly, in the resurrection we find not only a vindication of this renewed humanity brought about by Jesus's obedience but also an *affirmation of creation*. The resurrection shows us God's purpose for the world that he has made, for the resurrection is the first fruit of that purpose. In his 1968 book *Resurrection and the Moral Order*, Oliver O'Donovan said (and I think rightly) that our moral conduct and our moral sense must be based not only on creation, on how things are, but also on the resurrection, on how things ought to be.

It is often said that if Jesus is Lord at all, he must be Lord *of* all; and this brings me to the question of Christ and culture.

Jesus and culture: four models

This Jesus who has suffered and has now been raised and exalted: what is his relationship to the cultures in which we find ourselves? Of course, culture can be a very positive thing, a God-given thing. It can, as the second Vatican council said in the 1960s, enlarge the possibilities of refinement and development in human capacities and achievements. But culture also has another side to it, for since we are a fallen humanity, our cultures are also fallen. Self-evidently, it is all too easy to seesaw between too positive and too negative a view of human culture: what we need is a balanced view of how the Gospel can relate to culture. In the New Testament and later in the very early Church we find both an affirmation of culture and a critical attitude to it. The rational principle of the universe, the Logos incarnate in Christ, certainly provides grounds for some confidence in affirming many aspects of human society, human achievement, and human wisdom; but it also provides a critical principle that should prevent Christians from swallowing every cultural fad and fashion swirling around them. Richard Niebuhr, the 20th century American theologian has set out the different ways in which Christians have thought about the relationship of Christ to culture.

First of all, there is the *Christ of culture* where people find the Christian faith underpinning their cultural world – a faith that has, for better or for worse, produced the institutions, the customs, the laws, and the values of that culture. It has, moreover, provided a principle of criticism that has enabled culture to be critiqued in the light of Christ. I have argued that Britain is a very good example of such a situation if only it could remember its cultural roots, which it is steadfastly refusing to do at the moment. There are many other examples, and as Niebuhr points out, this understanding of culture is not to be identified only with western Christendom: it is also found in places like Ethiopia, Armenia or among the Maronites of Syria and Lebanon. More recently, as Professor Lamin Sanneh (a convert from Islam to Christian faith and now a professor at Yale University) has shown in his writings, there are many of the cultures in Africa that have become influenced by the Gospel.

Then, secondly, there is *Christ above culture* – that is, where society is based on the principles of natural law and reflects to some extent the divine will, but where people still yearn for the presence of the divine being himself. So revelation and grace are necessary to complete the nature of human society. It is a view that has been very influential, for example, in the Roman Catholic Church.

Thirdly, we have *Christ against culture*. I hope that here you will allow me a remark about our present situation, for it may be that in this country we are moving from the models of Christ *for* culture and Christ *of* culture to one of Christ *against* culture – for contemporary British culture seems to many Christians to be going in a wrong direction. There are many examples of this, and we should not be surprised that a dominant metaphor in Christian discourse is now changing from 'salt' to 'light'. Salt is effective when it is *dispersed* throughout whatever is being eaten or preserved, and our churches are very used to the salt metaphor as they try to work *with* the grain of society in performing valuable pastoral duties and that kind of thing. Light, though, is a *focus*, not a dispersant, and it may be that we are moving from the idea of being salt to that of becoming distinct spiritual and moral beacons of light in the approaching darkness.

And then, fourthly, we have *Christ as the transformer of culture*, so that when the Gospel arrives in any community or culture, it never arrives as a naked or impersonal ideal. It always arrives incarnate in a person, transforming and enfolding that culture within the work of God. When you think of the many untouchable people in India and of the humiliating conditions under which they lived in the caste system, the arrival of the Gospel and of the Christian church restored their dignity and opened their minds and hearts and spirits to God's work among them.

There are many similar examples. In a landmark address to the 1988 Lambeth Conference, the late Archbishop of the Anglican Church in Kenya, David Gitari, spoke of the transformational effects of the Gospel when it arrived among his people. It affirmed many of the things that were already there in their culture, for example their sense of solidarity, their sense of belonging in a community, and their finding within it an abundance of hospitality, spontaneity and creativity. All of these things were affirmed and enhanced by the coming of the Good News of Jesus Christ.

Of course, there were also some things about which the Gospel *didn't* have anything particular to say. Whether people should eat ugali or sausages and mash is something that the Gospel is silent about. And there were some things that the Gospel could tolerate for the time being. Gitari mentioned, for example, the custom among his people of men and women never sitting together in public meetings and even of having separate meetings. He also – controversially - mentioned polygamy as something that could be tolerated for a generation while the people were Christianised. But there were other things which the Gospel could not tolerate at all, such as the killing of twins because multiple births were supposed to be a curse. And cattle-rustling: you know, some of the people believed that all the cattle in the world belonged to them, so if someone took your cow, it was not really stealing. Quite a convenient doctrine to have!

Now, Archbishop Gitari has been attacked for a number of the things that he has said. Although the idea of *ubuntu*, or solidarity, was valuable in fostering and maintaining a sense of community among people, it was bad if it prevented the acceptance of the Good News by groups of people. In defending polygamy, Gitari was criticized for saying that there was no consistent trajectory about monogamy in the Bible. I think he was wrong about that: if you read the creation narratives, or what Malachi says about marriage in the Old Testament, or Jesus's teaching about marriage, or the teaching of St Paul, you would have to think that monogamy was absolutely the norm in the early churches. At the same time, though, I do think that what Gitari has said is illuminating for people in many different cultures as they seek to discern the things that the Gospel is affirming and the things that it is judging.

False and true religion

I maintain that culture cannot be understood without a proper understanding of religion, for culture is underpinned by religious ideas, customs and practices. Let us be clear that the Bible always condemns false religion. There is no acceptance of it. Thus, the hierarchical religion of the Canaanites, with the priest-king at its apex, was challenged by the egalitarianism of the early Israelites who, believing in one God, also believed that they were equal. So the oppressive hierarchical system was challenged and named. The same thing happened when the Israelites encountered the lack of respect for human dignity that characterised the permissive cults of Baal. Wherever there is idolatry, there is false religion, and the Bible condemns it.

Yet this is not the whole story, for we also find in the Bible some weighty moral figures who were not of the people of God, as it were, but who were acknowledged to have had some kind of spiritual awareness. I often give the example of Melchizedek, who as a Canaanite priest-king was the very kind of person that the Bible elsewhere condemns; yet Melchizadek brings bread and wine to the Patriarch Abraham and Abraham makes him an offering. Who was this Melchizedek? There is much reflection about him in the Bible later on. Many other such examples can be given: think of Job, Naaman, Nebuchadnezzar, Ruth, and so on

And there is more, for the Bible also shows God working even among those who were the enemies of Israel. The biblical history of the salvation of God's people is thus a reliable guide for seeing the work of God on a wider stage. As we well know, Jesus often elicited a faithful response from those who were not Jews. Remember what he said about the centurion's faith: 'I have not found such faith in Israel and many will come from east and west and sit at a table with Abraham and Isaac and Jacob'. Think too of the Samaritan woman, the Syrophoenician woman, and later on in the Acts of the Apostles, Cornelius.

How much the Christian mission depended on those god-fearing people who were to be found in the outer circles of the synagogues! Here is an acknowledgement that God has not left himself without witnesses, as St Paul testified in Lystra and in Athens. Paul's spirit was provoked within him at the idolatry he saw around him, yet still he was concerned to find some point of connection with the people he was addressing. Paul's quotes from the pagan poets originally referred to Zeus but I am told on good authority that, at the time of Paul, these quotations were understood by the Stoics and others to refer to the Logos.

This attitude was continued by the early fathers, particularly the apologists, Justin Martyr and Clement of Alexandria, who on the one hand were concerned to show the work of the universal Logos, God's Eternal Word, in exposing the falsehoods in human culture and human belief, yet on the other to acknowledge the Logos as the power that enables people to criticise their cultures and even their religions. In their writings, Justin and Clement accepted the elements of truth that there were in the philosophy and the practical morality of the Stoics. The Stoics were, for example, the first people to advocate the abolition of slavery. The Fathers were scathing about the falsehoods of pagan poetry; yet they noted that St Paul was able to quote from it. Pagan prophets are even pressed into the service of the Gospel by saying that, even in their darkness, they had anticipated the coming of Christ.

Being Christian within other religious traditions

As with culture, so with religion we have to be discriminating when we bring the Good News of Jesus Christ into a particular place to a particular people. Let me raise two questions about this and then I'll stop. One is the question of whether it is possible for people to be followers of Christ within their own non-Christian religious traditions. For many years I have debated this question with Phil Parshall, a missionary among Muslim people for almost half a century, who believes that it is possible within Islam for people to be Muslim Christians and to follow Christ within Islam.

The same claim is made by Mazhar Mallouhi, a Syrian Muslim who became a Christian but, finding that he was not welcome in an Arab-Christian community, decided to remain a follower of Christ within Islam. Is that possible? I have learnt a very great deal from Parshall and Mallouhi, but in the end I have to conclude that we are not saved in isolation. We are saved in the company of the people that God is saving for himself. I do acknowledge, however, that the Church has many weaknesses and makes many mistakes, but it needs to be enriched by people coming to Christ from other faiths. And they are enriched by coming into fellowship with other Christians, however difficult that may be.

Secondly, there is the question of whether it is possible for other religious traditions themselves to be transformed by the Christian Gospel. John V Taylor, who was a very distinguished predecessor of mine at the Church Mission Society, thought that it was. Today, for example, Hinduism is unrecognizable from the Hinduism of say 200 years ago because of its contact with Christianity. We see this in the monotheism of educated Hindus, in its treatment of women, and in the abolition of the caste system in modern India. Successive Hindu reformers like Raja Ram Mohan Roy, Rabindranath Tagore and Mahatma Gandhi himself have acknowledged this. M.M Thomas's book *The Acknowledged Christ of the Indian Renaissance*, published in 1970, is well worth reading on this, and so too is Kenneth Cragg, who committed his life to commending Christ according to the logic of Islam and was still writing at the time of his death just short of 100. Now, I personally think that any attempt to understand the fullness of God's revelation in Christ according to the logic of Islam is bound to fail, but this is not the time to go into that; I think one must admire the exercise without necessarily agreeing with it. It is certainly possible for religious traditions to be affected and changed by the Gospel; but how far this can go, and at what stage a more radical conversion is necessary, is an open question.

22816753R00047

Printed in Poland
by Amazon Fulfillment
Poland Sp. z o.o., Wrocław